The Grave Robber Next Door...
A Love Story

The True Story
Behind Naperville's Most Notorious Secret.

First Edition

Written by Kevin J. Frantz

Based on the research of
Kevin J. Frantz
and
Chuck Kennedy

The Grave Robber Next Door... A Love Story   First Edition © 2011 by Kevin J. Frantz. All rights reserved. No part of this book may be used, transmitted, or reproduced in any manner whatsoever, including live performance, Internet usage, without written permission from the author, except in the case of quotations embodied in critical articles, stories, and reviews.

Book cover design by Janice
Photo of Kevin on back cover by Elise Frantz
Edited by Janice
Published by Unrested Dead Publishing

Special thanks go out to the Naperville Library, Brian Ogg and the Naperville Historical Society, Alexander Felix, Beth Shields, Kirsten Tillman, The Paranormal Cops Team, Scott MacKay, Diane Ladley, Curt Morley, Denise Crosby, my beautiful wife Janice, and my unbelievable kids Jacob & Elise. And a special thanks goes out to my fellow researcher, Chuck Kennedy. Because without him the full story of Charles Hillegas would have never been completely told.

Printed in the United States of America

Visit Kevin's Ghost Tour online: HauntedNaperville.com
Visit Chuck Kennedy online: GhostsOfIllinois.com
Visit Alexander Felix online: WeGoParanormal.com

To share Naperville ghost stories, request investigations, ask questions, etc., Kevin can be reached at (630) 205-2664. Or, Info@NapervilleGhosts.com

The Grave Robber Next Door...
A Love Story

The True Story Behind
Naperville's Most Notorious Secret.

First Edition

Written by Kevin J. Frantz

Based on the research of
Kevin J. Frantz
and
Chuck Kennedy

Copyright © 2011 Kevin J. Frantz

All rights reserved.

ISBN-13: 978-1475241693
ISBN-10: 1475241690

TABLE OF CONTENTS

1 Introduction — Page 13

2 The Grave Robber Next Door (story only) — Page 23

3 Epilogue — Page 89

4 The Grave Robber Next Door (with evidence & commentary) — Page 103

5 The Lost Graves — Page 219

6 A Psychological Profile by Dr. Charles Kennedy — Page 227

7 Appendix — Page 237

The Grave Robber Next Door...
A Love Story

The True Story Behind
Naperville's Most Notorious Secret.

First Edition

Written by Kevin J. Frantz

Based on the research of
Kevin J. Frantz
and
Chuck Kennedy

Introduction

In Naperville, Illinois, for almost 100 years, people have discussed, debated, questioned, exaggerated, and drawn incorrect conclusions concerning the story of "Naperville's Grave Robber."
"Did he really exist?"
"Did he actually rob graves?"
"They say he force-fed his dead wife bananas hoping she wasn't dead."

"He was crazy, and crazy people do crazy things."
"He was a senile octogenarian who couldn't handle his wife's demise."
"There never was a grave robber in Naperville, the whole story is pure folklore."
Etc. etc.

So, did the grave robber really exist? I'm happy to say that he most certainly DID exist. And he did commit a vile act of grave desecration. Of course, the question then becomes: IF he did exist, why isn't the story better understood? Why are the facts so shrouded? If something so strange actually happened on the streets of Naperville, how come no one knows the true story? Well, as sad as it sounds, the problem is: *Naperville.*

Naperville has a habit of sweeping things that it doesn't like "under the rug" - *if you can't see the problem, it doesn't exist. Right?* It started a long time ago. Napervillians of old believed that if you stop talking about something, eventually it's forgotten and for all practical purposes, *it never happened.* This type delusional thinking continues even to this day.

As an example, in May of 1979 Naperville's "Naperville Sun" newspaper published a story about The Historical Society's "Plaquing" of the historic home where the grave robber brought the dead body, but the story *didn't even mention the grave-robbing episode*! They mentioned lots of fascinating history that surrounded the house, but not so much as a syllable was uttered concerning the grave robbing that took place at the house! *Grave robbing, what grave robbing??* And so it goes...

The local papers routinely give Naperville's bad news very limited, if any, coverage. The local papers have always trumpeted Naperville's triumphs, and buried her blunders. - And the story of Naperville's Grave Robber is a textbook example of this lunacy.

The actual event of the grave robbing happened in May of 1912. That means that this year, 2012, we celebrate the 100th anniversary of the event. Don't you find it peculiar that in 100 years of Naperville history no one has bothered to set the record straight on this queer story? Instead of discussing the facts of the event, the event was pushed under a rug. As a result, people made up new "facts." The story became fodder for kids to embellish during story times on Halloween. Of course, over the years, the actual facts of the story grew more faint and confused, while the folklore of it limped along refusing to completely die.

Note: there was an account of the Grave Robber story in a book called Haunted Naperville, by Diane Ladley (later changed to: Naperville's Haunted Memories). The "true" Grave Robber account in that book was completely fallacious and only served to compound the confusion.

I find it interesting that the true story of Naperville's Grave Robber will finally be told, here on these pages, on this, the 100th year anniversary of the gruesome event.

The grave robber story required incredible amounts of digging (pardon the pun,) to get to the truth; the whole story wasn't available in any one place. Many pieces had to be assembled to get the full picture into focus; and those pieces came from many different sources. My fellow investigator in this project is Chuck Kennedy. Chuck is a medical professional, author, researcher, and paranormal investigator; his expertise and patience have been, and continue to be, invaluable in unraveling the true story of Naperville's Grave Robber. (Chuck is available at GhostsOfIllinois.com).

The Grave Robber Next Door

Before we tackle the true story of the Grave Robber, let's look at a couple versions of the story that have been told by many people (including myself!) on the streets of Naperville...

Story One:

In 1864, a wealthy hardware store owner in Naperville had a house built on the southeast corner of Jefferson and Front Streets (Front Street is today Ellsworth Street). The house was a wedding gift to one of his sons. The house still stands today, and is commonly referred to as the Baumgartner house.

The doorway on the right side is actually a stairway, a steep stairway that leads up to the second floor. The second floor window, far right, was a window in the master bedroom of the house.

As the story goes, the man and his new wife moved into the wedding present house. They enjoyed a very happy life together for many years. Then, in about 1897, the man awoke one morning to discover that his beautiful wife had died during the night. There was a quick funeral for her in the parlor of the house. Then her pine coffin was loaded onto a horse-drawn hearse that brought her to the Naperville Cemetery, just a few blocks from his house, where she was laid to rest.

The man came back home alone and distraught. He sat down at the kitchen table, and noticed a bowl of bananas that someone had left for him. That's when it occurred to him that maybe his wife wasn't dead after all - maybe she had just passed out? Maybe all she needs is something healthy to eat! - *Like... bananas.*

So, quickly, by the cover of night, he ran to the barn, secured a shovel and wheelbarrow, and headed off to the Naperville Cemetery.

The dirt was of course still loose over his wife's grave as he sank the shovel in. He tossed the shovel-full of dirt off to the side and continued relentlessly until he'd reached her coffin, several feet under ground. There, he pried open the lid, and removed his bride from her burial place. He gently placed her in the wheelbarrow and made his way back home.

When he got home his intent was to bring her up the stairway to their bed, to get her under the covers where she could warm up - she was sooooooo cold. But try as he might, he couldn't get her up those steep, steep, stairs. He kept falling into the walls - crash, boom. They fell down the stairs over and over again. After numerous attempts, he quit and brought her instead to the kitchen. There he sat her at the dining table.

He took a seat opposite her and offered her a banana. Her snarled hair hung in her pale face as she sat quietly, head tilted to one side. She didn't answer. He reasoned that she was too malnourished to even speak. He'd better hurry and feed her ...*something*. He grabbed a banana from the bowl and peeled it. He offered it to her – no response. He slid his chair in closer to her and kissed her on the cheek almost apologetically. He then pried open her mouth and stuck the banana in an inch or two and pushed it down onto her bottom teeth to break it off. He smiled, sighing, "That was a good bite, now just chew it." Unfortunately, the banana piece sat motionless in her purple mouth. He then stuck his fingers in and pushed the banana piece down her throat. He was surprised that it slid down so easily! He quickly had her "bite" another chunk and he pushed it too down the hatch. He continued until all the bananas were gone. Then he sat down across from her and waited for the fruit to revitalize her. As night deepened he gradually fell to sleep while waiting.

In the morning, two of the widower's children came by to check on dad only to find him sound asleep at the kitchen table – with mom. *Still dead.*

Needless to say, mom was reburied and dad went to a mental hospital. He died a short time later and joined his wife in eternity.

But, they say... sometimes, in that old house, in the middle of the night, strange sounds can be heard coming from that steep old stairway even to this day. Sounds of banging and crashing, like someone is falling into the walls while trying to carry a load that is much, much, too heavy for them...

* * *

A fun story, but very little of it is accurate. It is true that there was a man and a wife. And, the house was a wedding gift, she did die and he did dig her up and bring her home. Other than that though this story is complete fabrication – even the location. *Sorry.*

Story Two:

Diane Ladley's "true" account from her book: Haunted Naperville? (Later renamed: Naperville's Haunted Memories) Material copyright Diane Ladley, Arcadia Publishing.

According to Miss Ladley:

Back in 1870 the beautiful home located at 105 Ellsworth was built as a wedding present for Charles Hillegas and his wife Sarah. Charles and Sarah were happy in their home, and raised a family of two sons and a daughter. Charles enjoyed mixing herbs and potions into new elixirs that he hoped would benefit mankind.

Then, in 1898, Sarah died from a short sudden illness. Charles made a vow that he'd create a formula to bring her back from the dead. After 18 years of experiments with dead chickens, Charles had a formula he felt good about. He killed a chicken, crammed some of his formula down its gullet, and waited.... Soon it came to life! Charles had done it; he found the secret of life!

So he went to the cemetery and dug up his wife – who he'd buried 18 years earlier. He put what was left of her in a wheelbarrow and took her home to his mother's barn on Ellsworth Street.

There, he fed her the life-giving potion.

Nothing happened.

No one discovered them in the barn for almost two weeks. But soon the law showed up and Charles ended up being sent to a padded room on the east coast where he belonged.

It's a cute story. The problem though is that it isn't true! For Miss Ladley to publish this account as the factual true story of the grave-robbing event was grossly irresponsible.

So, what then is the true story of Naperville's Grave Robber? It gives Chuck Kennedy and I great pleasure, here on the 100th anniversary of the event, to publish for the first time, in the history of Naperville, the true account of Naperville's Grave Robber.

It comes as a surprise to most people that the story of Naperville's Grave Robber is actually a *Love Story*. Oh, it has its share of the macabre, and deception, violence, denial, greed, desperation, and magic. But at its core, Love is the catalyst that drove the nightmare into reality. *Love*.

Note: Because this story has been so subjected to so much misinformation over the years, it is important to Chuck and I that we share not only the fascinating story, but the *evidence for the story as well*. Unfortunately, if we share the story and evidence laterally, the evidence will bog down the story! Therefore, in this book, we will share the Grave Robber story in two phases. First, we'll share with you the true story of Naperville's Grave Robber, focusing *only on the story itself*. Then, following the story, we'll share the story again but this 2nd time we'll share with you the evidence as well, as we move through the story. In addition to evidence, we'll share with you how we arrived logically at the conclusions we did when evidence either contradicted itself or was lacking.

We believe this is the best approach for an historical account of this magnitude and importance to Naperville's history.

Following the 2nd telling will be two additional sections relating to the story:
1) The Discovery of the Lost Graves

2) The Grave Robber's Psychological Profile

The Appendix included herein contains scans of information important to this story, such as: obituaries, newspaper stories, etc.

And, now, the True Story of Naperville's Grave Robber Next Door...

The Grave Robber Next Door... *A Love Story*

It was a stifling day in Naperville, Illinois, 1862. William Hillegas, age 22, stood sweltering in the Zion church of Naperville on this, his wedding day – July 3rd. His beautiful bride, Maria Hartman, held his quivering hand as the ceremony began. William glanced back over his left shoulder, out into the pews – there, sat his parents-in-law, Adam and Susana, as well as his father, Joseph, all smiling back at him with pride. How he wished his mom could be here. '*Has it really been two years since the good Lord took her from us?*' he thought. He missed her more today than ever. She, too, would be so proud of him. He fought back a tear and turned to his bride. The look in his eyes told her what he was thinking; she squeezed his hand tighter in support for his loss. He felt better. He was in good hands.

William and Maria immediately settled down in Naperville to begin their new life together. The years were filled with blessing. William's job at the Fridley Hardware Store in Naperville became a dream come true when he partnered with Louis Rieche and together they purchased the Fridley store on Jefferson Street. William was finally a business owner, a goal he'd long hoped and worked for. Then on August 3rd, 1863, William and Maria welcomed their first child; a beautiful daughter, they name her Ida May. When William's father saw the family growing he offered to buy a house for William and Maria as a wedding present. He could see that they were going to outgrow their current dwelling very soon. William accepted the kind offer, and the question became - where to build it?

The proud parents were very fond of Naperville's affluent east side. Which was fine, because, as a successful businessman in Naperville, that's where William and his family *belonged*. A modest and beautiful house was designed, complete with rising turret. They chose a plot of land across Benton Street from Sts. Peter and Paul Catholic Church, on the southeast corner of Benton and Front. They couldn't wait to move in.

This is the home built for William Hillegas as a wedding gift. It is on the southeast corner of Benton and Ellsworth Streets.

That Damn Sense of Duty

Maria had fallen in love with William's strength. His character, she knew, was impeccable; his confidence, unshakable; his concern for others, honorable. He lived his life with a Christian drive to do the right thing regardless of personal cost. His life motto, printed on his heart, was: *better to suffer wrong than do wrong*. But she always knew, perhaps only in the back of her mind, that someday his sense of duty would be a sacrifice they'll all be asked to make. She knew it would happen *eventually* – she just didn't expect it to happen *so quickly*.

William Hillegas

As the Civil War raged on, the need for Union soldiers grew urgent. The plea for manpower soon reached Naperville and the heart of 24-year-old William Hillegas. Immediately his impulse was to help. Knowing that this decision could lead him to the ultimate sacrifice didn't discourage him at all; *it, after all, was his duty.* Surely, his wife and daughter will understand that. Maria was never more proud of him.

In 1864, William joined the war effort. He was a member of the Company D, 156th Illinois Infantry. He served until the close of the war, in April of 1865. He served bravely and received an Honorable Discharge. He returned to Naperville, his family, his business, and his new home.

And growing, and growing...

With the nation reeling from the assassination of President Lincoln, William continued to apply himself to growing his business, and growing his family. As 1866 gave way to 1867, the good news that Maria was again with child brought immeasurable joy to the Hillegas home. Maria, now being referred to as Mary, worked hard to be a devout Christian wife, neighbor, and mother, as she prepared for the second addition to the Hillegas clan.

On July 25th, 1867, William's second child - a son - Charles William Hillegas, was born in that simple gray turreted wedding present. It didn't take long for William and Mary to realize that they needed more room for their growing crew, and besides, business was good. They agreed that a larger, more spacious, home is required. Something with high ceilings, comfortable rooms, farm area, perhaps a barn. *They will have the best house on Front Street.* Yes, this was a good idea. William went to work immediately.

Desiring to stay in Naperville's east side, they purchased a large piece of vacant land a block south of their current house, on the northwest corner of Front and Liberty Street. It had ample space for building; the east edge of the property ran along Front Street and continued all the way to the west, to Court Street. Public Square Park sat beautifully behind the property, just to the west.

The design was coming together; it looked like they'd be finished and moved in by early 1870. And just in time too - Mary is again with child, due in 1870.

When the house was completed it was beyond their dreams. It stood beautifully on the corner of Front and Liberty Street, a testament to the Hillegas success story. It was a stately three-story red brick building with a large veranda that bordered the front and side of the house. The interior of the home was as equally impressive as the exterior, boasting comforts that made it the epitome of 19th century living: 14 rooms, six chimneys, stove heating, as well as two parlors - separated by heavy double doors. In every way the house and grounds were stunningly beautiful.

A large barn sat comfortably in the rear of the property along Court St.

The Hillegas house in about 1875. Note the large barn in the rear of the property.

Naperville, Our Hometown

Once comfortably moved in, the Hillegas family took their rightful place among Naperville's influential. The Hillegas Hardware store continued to grow, adding products such as: butcher knives, cooking & heating stoves, scales, spring buggies, food cutters, corn shellers, and bob sleighs. At this time Hillegas Hardware is also recognized as one of Naperville's most efficient and up-to-date offices. Being a devout Christian man with a Christian family, William would do no business on Sundays.

Through the 1800s, Naperville itself was growing as gravel roads were being extended in all directions. As well, Naperville was becoming a booming business center, adding among its offerings: Milling, Farm Machinery Manufacture, Buggy Making, Blacksmithing, Breweries, Hospitality, Furniture Manufacturing, Undertaking, Saddle Making, Tailoring, Winemaking, Cigar Manufacturing, Livery and Stables, Doctors, Surgeons, Quarrying, Dentists, Toy Factory, Photographers, Movie Shows, and Fine Dining. Stores opened to service the town, selling: Insurance, Jewelry, Books, Shoes, Drugs, Music Machines, Hunting Supplies, Oysters, Produce, Meat, and Gifts. There was even an American Indian who opened a storefront shooting gallery on Main Street.

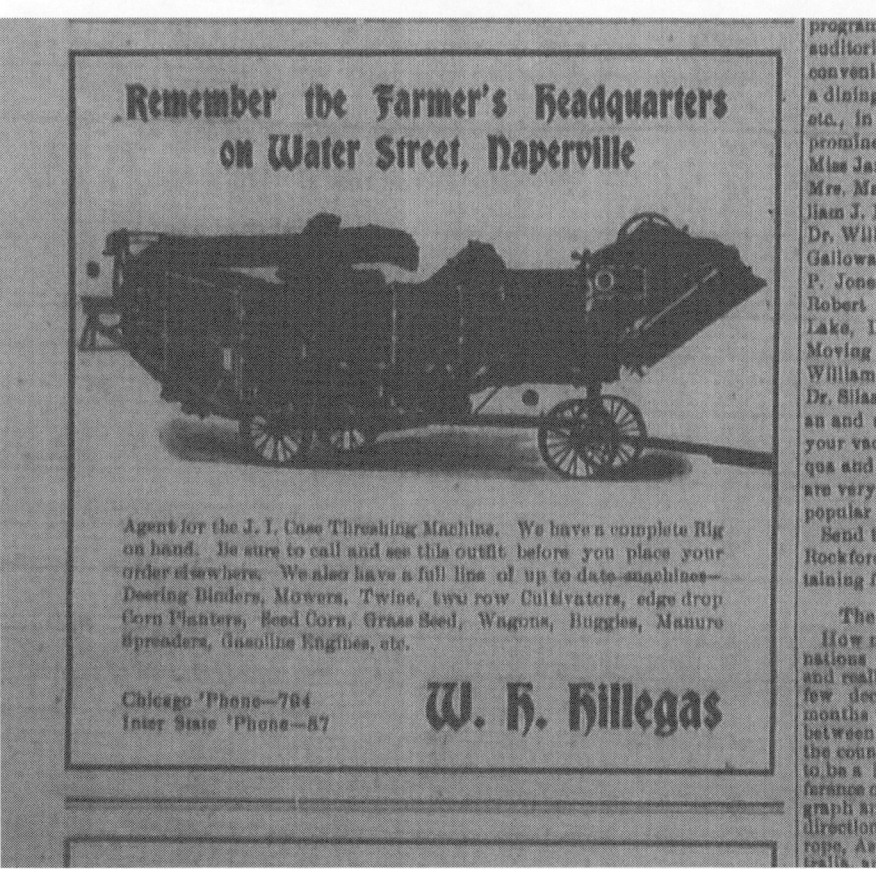

Hillegas Hardware ad - 1904

There were new businesses and opportunities everywhere. And of course, the perennial polar opposites were everywhere too: Churches and Saloons. Both were going gangbusters. Curiously, in the newspapers of the day, ads for saloons read: **All Welcome**. Ads for churches read: **Citizens Welcome. Strangers** *Generally* **Welcome**. Some things never change...

The river that ran through Naperville was quite a bit different at that time than it is today. Namely, it was much wider; was known to have rattlesnakes; and, in the mid 1880s, was infested with Mink. They were causing major headaches, especially for the chicken farmers - Mink do like chicken evidentially. Many dealers were paying handsomely for the skins of the rascals.

It was in this atmosphere that William was raising his family: a daughter and two sons. Home life for the Hillegas family was happy overall. William raised his family with devout Christian principals. Mary was a kind and caring mother, wife, friend, and neighbor. She was led to Christ in her early youth and lived her life with a strong personality, sterling character, and Christ-likeness. She filled her life with ministries of love and kindness; she even provided a couple of her favorite recipes to the locally produced hometown cookbooks.

> THE NAPERVILLE COOK BOOK. 47
>
> SNOW CAKE.
>
> One cup sugar, one-half cup butter, one-half cup sweet milk, two cups flour, whites of four eggs, two teaspoons baking powder.   Mrs. W. H. Hillegas.

From a Naperville cookbook, circa 1902

William and Mary's eldest child, daughter Ida, grew up with the values of the time for a young lady - she married young to a local boy, Simon Schaefle, and began raising her own family. Harvey, the youngest, showed early the same drive for success that his father had. He endeavored to learn the ropes of business from his father by helping out in the new, larger, Hillegas Hardware store on Water Street. He joined the Naperville Hook and Ladder (similar to a fire department). And, at the age of just 15, would travel to Chicago everyday for lessons in Architecture, his hope to one day be an architect.

William's middle child, and eldest son, Charles, had an independent streak. He wasn't so much interested in following dear old dad's footsteps in the hardware business. But, the local drug store with its endless array of miracle potions and elixirs enchanted him. He was an intelligent lad, and enjoyed teaming up with his brother Harvey in the mixing of herbs and roots into new concoctions. A bout with pneumonia, in February of 1886, only strengthened his resolve to break new ground in this intriguing arena called apothecary. Charles was out of Naperville, away at school, for his early teen years.

Dawn of a New Century

As America prepared for the changing of the century the Hillegas family continued to apply themselves to their business and family-related goals. Always striving to be at the forefront, Hillegas Hardware was one of Naperville's most efficient and progressive businesses. Hillegas Hardware was one of just 20 Naperville businesses to have telephone service in the early 1900s.

Then, in 1899, Harvey Hillegas married a beautiful young lady named Jenette (her friends call her Jinnie). In attendance at the wedding was a Hillegas-family friend, a young lady that Charles had been smitten-with for a long time, her name was Jessie - Jessie Robateene Massey. She lived in nearby Will County and was married to an angry and abusive husband, George F. Scollard. Jessie had been born in England in 1876 and came to America with her family when she was just a young girl. One of the first things her parents did when they arrived in America was to marry off their 15-year-old flower, Jessie. The marriage was on December 11, 1891. The man they chose made life unbearable for Jessie. It broke Charles' heart every time he'd talk to her about it. Her eyes were so sad; how he wished he could help her. *If only they had married her off to Charles, she'd be treated like a Queen...*

On the day of Harvey's wedding, Charles saw Jessie enter the house and immediately approached her. As he spoke to her he realized that there was something different about her – her smile seemed more natural, her adorable English accent seemed more... upbeat. He didn't have to ask her why, she offered it – "I'm going to leave George. I can't take it anymore. Eight years with that pig is enough. I know it's horrible, but I'm going to get a divorce from him. I've never felt so alive. He doesn't know yet. I'm afraid of him so I'm going to run away and stay with friends in Indianapolis till it's over." Charles saw this situation as his chance; Jessie could now be *his wife*. He didn't say anything to her then, but his mind immediately began making plans...

The Line in the Sand

In the days that followed, Charles realized that the first step in making Jessie his wife was to secure the support of mom and dad. He sat down with them in the parlor. He explained the situation, and asked for their blessing. To his surprise, he was met with complete rejection. William erupted, "Absolutely not! Marrying a divorced woman will make you an adulterer – the Bible is clear on this fact. It is her duty to remain with her husband. Her actions are shameful and will under no circumstances be tolerated in the Hillegas family. She has partnered with the devil and no son of mine will have any part of it." William stormed out of the house. Mary remained at the table and wept. Charles went upstairs to his room. He counted out some cash he'd tucked away. He packed a bag and made his way to the train station.

It seemed like forever waiting for a train, but soon a light was faintly visible down the tracks to the east. He didn't care where it was destined; he just wanted to get as far from Naperville as he could. As he boarded he asked the conductor how far he could go with the money he had. The conductor counted it out and told him that the train goes all the way to Seattle Washington, and Charles had enough to get there. Charles handed the money over and plopped down in the seat. He watched out the window as Naperville grew more distant, he angrily sighed, "Damn hillbilly dump."

Westward Ho

Charles didn't have a specific destination in mind. He and his brother had often talked about living in the west; Harvey was targeting Los Angeles. Charles didn't have a preference and at this point anyplace that wasn't Naperville would suffice. Charles was a few days into his exodus, when he heard the conductor call out that the next stop was Helena Montana. Charles had heard of that place, lots of silver prospecting going on as he recalled. He decided to disembark there.

Charles set his bag down on the Helena Depot platform, and stretched; it had been a long time just sittin'. It was clear that this was a busy place, not the quiet hovel that Naperville was. He sought lodging and settled down for a good night's sleep.

As the days passed Charles realized that if you weren't a silver miner or John this just wasn't the place to settle down. It was a progressive city though, that's for sure; every convenience and pleasure was to be had. It wasn't for him; he decided to continue his travels on through to Seattle.

Making a New Home

Seattle was much more to Charles' tastes. It was big and beautiful, full of opportunity and friendly people, and the ocean... Charles had never seen anything else like it. He loved it. Yes, Seattle would do nicely, and besides, he couldn't get much further from Naperville if he tried. One of Charles' first orders of business was to get in touch with Jessie. She didn't know that he had left Naperville and was now living practically in the Pacific Ocean.

Charles would take odd jobs to pay the bills, all the while keeping an eye on the post - waiting for a letter from Indianapolis. It had been months since he'd written to Jessie. He explained to her what had happened with his parents. He explained how he didn't care what they or their Bible thought of him. He loved her more than anything, and he wanted her to come be with him forever. He hoped that she felt the same way. He waited for a response. And he waited.

With each passing day the tight feeling in his chest would grow more uncomfortable with the realization that maybe he'd made a mistake. Doubts began to set in; maybe she didn't love or want him. He looked out the boarding house window, a fall breeze was blowing the multicolored leaves along the ground; he wondered if she'd ever really be his.

1900

With the new century Charles was still hopeful for a life with Jessie. He'd sent several letters over the last year without a response from her.

Then it happened.

Tucked away in his daily mail was a tattered envelope. He didn't give it much notice until he spotted the return address city: Indianapolis Indiana. He threw the other letters on the desk and sat on the edge of his bed near the window. He looked at the outside of the envelope, thinking, '*so that's what her handwriting looks like...*" He gently ran his fingertips over the ink for a few seconds.

He flipped it over and ripped the envelope open. He removed a letter, folded in thirds. He eagerly unfolded it, his eyes quickly scrolled to the bottom, and his heart skipped a beat. It was there - she'd signed the letter: Love, Jessie.

With renewed enthusiasm he read the letter in full. She apologized for taking so long to write. But, she explained, the divorce process had been much more difficult than she anticipated; her husband had been much more resistant than she anticipated; her family much less supportive than she had anticipated - the last year had been a nightmare. The only peace she got came from Charles' letters. They were the light at the end of her tunnel. Charles was the only person who understood, the only person not condemning her. She knew in her heart that they belonged together. But, she asked, "how?" They were now a million miles from each other.

Charles quickly wrote back to her with a plan: he was coming to get her, and bring her back to Seattle. Here they could start over, both of them, together...

A New Life Begins

In late October 1901, Charles arrived in Indiana to meet Jessie. They immediately boarded a westbound train to take them back to Seattle to get married. On the way, they discussed their life together. Charles' heart would beat faster just hearing Jessie speak; her eyes would twinkle when she gazed at him. They couldn't wait to be man and wife.

Charles suggested that they not wait until Seattle to get married; he knew of a city where they could get married, honeymoon, and celebrate their new life. The city, he said, was near Helena, Montana; it was called Butte. In was in Silver Bow County. Jessie smiled and threw her arms around him.

On Friday, November 1st, 1901, the train pulled into the Helena depot. Charles and Jessie disembarked and headed for the courthouse building for a license and a quick wedding ceremony. Charles is 34, Jessie 23.

The courthouse in Silver Bow County, Montana, in 1901

But, before Jessie allowed Charles to say, "I do," there was something very important she needs Charles to know about her...

Jessie led Charles to a bench in the courthouse entryway. They sat down, close to each other. She started to cry. "I should have told you earlier, I'm so sorry."
Charles' heart was breaking as he concluded that she didn't love him after all.
Jessie sniffled, and rubbed a tear from her eye, "We can't get married, I'm sorry..."
Charles felt like the his world was ending, "Why? I love you Jess. I love you..."
Jessie nodded as if she understood, saying, "We can't, I'm still married to George."
Charles pushed back, perplexed, "I thought.... the divorce?"
"It never happened. I tried! Honest. But without help... I couldn't do it alone. It was so hard. I tried... I wanted to tell you before... I'm sorry. I'm so sorry..."
Charles took a deep breath as he reached for Jessie's hand. As he kissed it gently he asked, "Do you still love George?"
Jessie's eyes were red from crying as she pushed her hair out of her face, confessing, "God, no."
Charles nodded. Then whispered, "And you love me?"
"More than anything."
Charles smiled. "Then we belong together. Divorced or not, Jessie will you still marry me?"
Jessie laughed, "I don't think they'll let us do that!"
"When we go in for the license, just tell them that you are divorced, they'll believe you."
"You'll be marrying a married woman."
Charles let out a frustrated sigh, "Dad practically sold me for fertilizer for marrying a divorced woman, I wonder what he'd say about a married woman?"
Jessie kissed Charles, and whispered in his ear, "I'm divorced in my heart..."

The Marriage License of Charles and Jessie, 1901.

After the ceremony Charles and Jessie began celebrating in Helena. Jessie found herself growing fond of the place; it was exciting and vibrant. She had been cooped up in small towns for too long. She asked Charles if he wouldn't mind staying in Helena for a while. What was the hurry to get to Seattle? Charles wasn't fond of Helena, but he'd do anything for Jessie. They found a boarding room and settled down, *for a few years anyway,* Charles thought.

For the next few years Charles would write letters in an attempt to smooth things over with his parents. Mom wrote back explaining that she missed him very much. Dad wasn't quite so understanding - his devout Christian principals were unwavering in his insistence that his son was now an adulterer, something he was completely unable to accept or condone.

Hillegas Hardware on Water Street, in Naperville, Illinois, early 1900s

Jessie had written to her parent's hoping that they could find peace in the fact that she is finally, for the first time on her life, happy. There was no reply. Then there was the ex-husband and his propensity to violence and anger. There was always that feeling – and both of them felt it – that at any time Jessie's ex-husband would show up at their door waving a gun; for this reason they kept a very low profile. If that man loved Jessie even a fraction of what Charles did, there was nothing in the world that could stop him from finding her.

* * *

A Message Arrives

It was Monday morning, April 30th, 1906. There was knock on the door. It was the delivery of a telegram.

* * * * *

SENT: NAPERVILLE, ILLINOIS   USA   29, APRIL 1906

RECEIVER: HILLEGAS, CHARLES   HELENA, MONTANA

MSG: PLEASE COME HOME -(STOP)-
    FATHER DIED LAST NIGHT -(STOP)-

    MOTHER INCONSOLABLE -(STOP)-
    ASKING FOR YOU -(STOP)-

HARVEY HILLEGAS   6:45AM

* * * * *

W. H. Hillegas Summoned.

Citizens were surprised last Sunday night to hear that death had claimed our townsman, W. H. Hillegas. Heart failure was the immediate cause of death. Funeral services will be held from Zion church Thursday morning, May 3d, at 10 o'clock.

Actual newspaper announcement 1906

Charles didn't say anything. In stunned shock, his hand went limp and the paper dropped to the ground. He vacantly backed away from the door. Jessie picked up the paper and read it. Without commenting she set it on a table. Then she put her arms around Charles. After a moment, she whispered, "He was a good man."

Charles stared off in the distance while nodding in agreement. "I should go see Mom."

"Yes."

That day Charles was on the train bound for Naperville.

On Wednesday, May 2nd, Charles arrived in Naperville. He walked the few blocks from the depot on 4th Avenue to his mother's house on Front Street. Many members of the family were already there, comforting Mary. Charles was met with a cool reception as he walked into the house. His brother Harvey was there with his wife Jenette, along with Charles' sister Ida and her husband Simon. Other neighbors and members of Naperville's government and business community were also present. They all knew Charles, and the conditions under which he left his family. He didn't mind their opinions, besides they were right – he'd traded the love and acceptance of his family and hometown for the love of a divorced "sinner" named Jessie. And if he had it to do over again, he'd make the exact same decisions. Jessie was alive and vibrant; these people were small-minded and petty. He'd do anything to have Jessie with him; giving up Naperville and his family was a small price to pay. He hugged his mother and went up to his room to be alone.

William's funeral was held the next day, Thursday, May 3rd, 1906, partly under the supervision of the G.A.R. -The acronym stood for the Grand Army of the Republic, of which William was a member. (The G.A.R. was a fraternal organization of honorably discharged Union Civil War veterans).

The funeral was a large affair. William was waked in the front parlor of the house he'd built 36 years earlier. 40 comrades of the G.A.R. served as pallbearers and escort. The floral tributes were appropriate, varied, and beautiful. Because of William's influence and respect in the community, representatives from every church and level of society were in attendance for the service in the Zion church, as well, no business was allowed to be transacted, in Naperville, during William's funeral service.

Later at the graveside, the Grand Army burial service closed the obsequies of one who would long be remembered fondly and lovingly.

The Talk that Changed Everything

As the funeral attendees dispersed from the graveside, Harvey approached Charles, "Have you got a minute to talk?"
Charles squinted at the morning sun shining through the trees. He continued walking and sighed a reluctant "Sure."
Harvey sensed the halfhearted attention and stepped in front of Charles to stop him. He looked him in the eye, "How long are you planning to stay in town?"
Charles looked around at the people leaving, he furled his brow, "Well, I'm not very welcome around here, but I'll stay as long as mom wants me to."
Harvey asked, "A few days?"
Charles snapped, "I don't know. Why do you care?"
Harvey looked over at his wife standing near William's open grave. She made eye contact with him and seemed to be losing patience waiting for him. Harvey took Charles by the arm and led him under a tree, away from his wife's view. He said, "I've been working for the last few month's with the artificial incubation of chickens, it's a fascinating science."
Charles smiled mockingly, "Seems somewhat beneath a Hillegas, -to keep company with filthy foul like a common... I don't know... farmer?"
"I agree. Dad wanted it. He thought there was money to be made with it."
"Maybe he was right."
"Maybe he was." He glanced at his father's newly dug grave, "Doesn't much matter anymore, does it?"
Charles shrugged his shoulders indifferently.
Harvey continued, "Besides, I think that whatever money dad was after, it is small potatoes compared to a discovery I inadvertently stumbled on with those filthy birds."
"Teach them to talk, did you?"
"No. Listen –"
Charles interrupted, "Good, they'd probably be foul-mouthed anyway."
Harvey rolled his eyes in disgust at the lame attempt at humor, "Do you remember those ridicules potions you and I used to experiment with?"
Charles got defensive, "They weren't ridicules. We had some worthwhile elixirs in there."

Harvey held up his hand as it to say 'enough'. "Sorry brother but they were ridicules. That is to say, all but one."

Charles was curious. "What are you getting at?"

"Sometimes, lately, when I was bored, I would go through our old notes, duplicate the potions, and feed them to the chickens, just to see how they would react. Most of the time nothing would happen. But, we had one mixture that was mostly banana, do you remember it?"

"Vaguely, yes."

"In our notes you wrote that it *was a pick-me-up potion. It was supposed to give massive amounts of energy to the weary.* So, I mixed a batch and ate some of it myself. I felt a bit dizzy from it. Then, using some of the leftover, I added a few more ingredients and gave some of if to one of the chickens."

Charles snapped, "And?"

"It died."

"It died?"

"Yeah. It was completely dead. I held it up, shook it, dunked it in water, nothing revived it. I had killed it with the new banana mixture!"

Charles was less than impressed. He snapped, sarcastically, "So, if everybody in America suddenly needs a quick way to kill all their chickens, they can buy our new banana potion to do it and we'll get rich?"

"No. Listen, I threw the dead chicken into a box thinking that I'd come back to him later and give it to mom to prepare him for a dinner. But, when I came back to get him a few hours later, he was alive!"

"So it was never really dead."

"No! It was dead. I'm positive!"

"How can a dead chicken come back to life? It doesn't make sense!"

"I thought the same thing. So, I killed a different chicken. Then, I crammed some of the banana potion down its throat."

"And?" Charles asked, losing patience.

"I waited."

"For what?"

"I didn't know..." Harvey took a deep breath, "A couple minutes later, it started moving."

Charles threw up his hands, "I've had enough. This is absurd." He started walking briskly toward Main Street. After a few seconds he turned back toward Harvey, shouting, "I'll be at the Pre-Emption House saloon, I need a drink!"

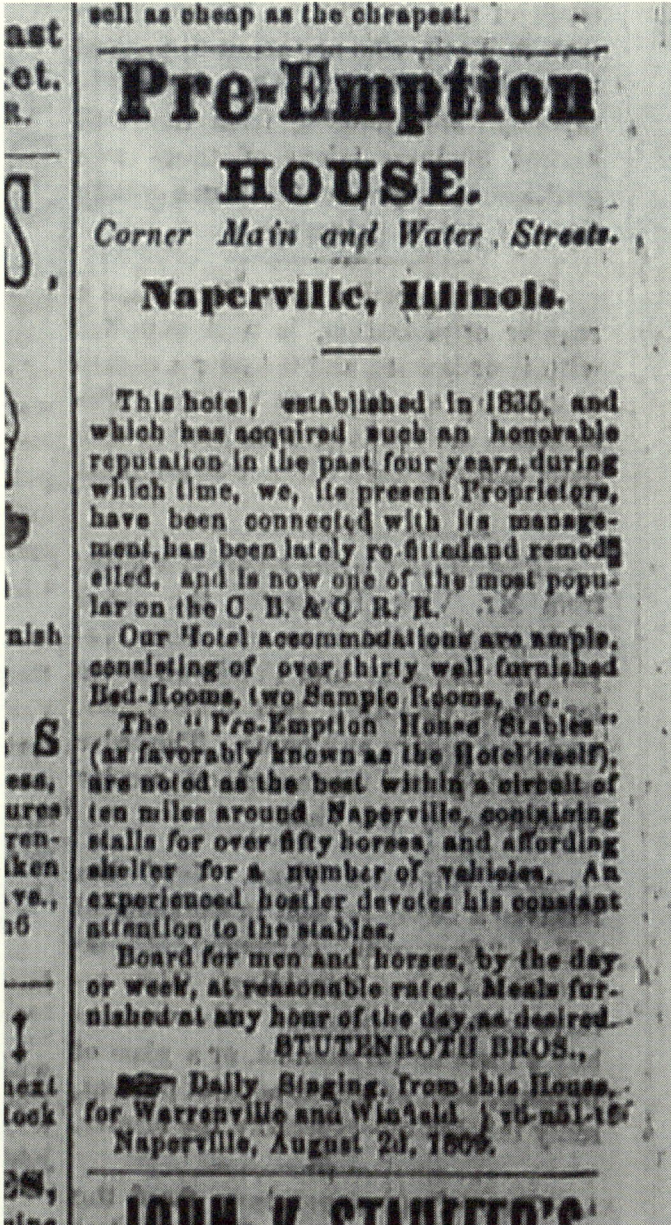

Pre-Emption House ad – late 1800s

Charles has Unbelievable News

The Pre-Emption House was a Naperville saloon, hotel, restaurant, and stable all rolled into one. Located on the southeast corner of Main and Jackson, The Pre-Emption House was a popular stop for locals and travelers alike.

Charles entered the saloon and sat himself down at the bar. The bartender recognized him and announced to the entire place, "Hey! If it isn't old Charley Hillegas, come to pay us a visit!" Charles shook his head is disbelief, "Can I just get a whiskey, please? It's only 11am and it's already a rotten day."
The bartender poured a tall one, "I know, Chuck. Your daddy was a great man he'll be missed. This one is on me."
Charles raised the glass in toast to the bartender's generosity. As he drank it down, a handful of locals approached Charles, patted him on the back, and expressed their sorrow for his loss. Charles went through the motions.
"So Chuck, how's life in the wide open west?"
"It's quite a bit different than Naperville that's for sure."
"So, will you and Harvey be taking over the business of Hillegas Hardware?"
Charles laughed, "I'll be heading back home in a few days. I don't know about Harvey, we haven't discussed the store. He'll probably open a funeral parlor, if I know him!"
"The Beidelman brothers funeral parlor might have a problem with that! They hate competition!"
"Oh, my brother wouldn't be competing with them. He doesn't bury the dead; he brings them back to life! He says he's got a magic potion that brings things back from the dead!"
The entire saloon was now laughing and making fun of Harvey and the Hillegas Banana Potion. "Hey Charles, what makes you Hillegas boys think anyone would want to bring back their dead? Especially my mother in law!!"
The whole of the saloon was having a great time at the expense of Charles, Harvey, and a crazy story about a life-restoring banana potion. In the days that followed the whole town was laughing about the banana potion at the Hillegas place.

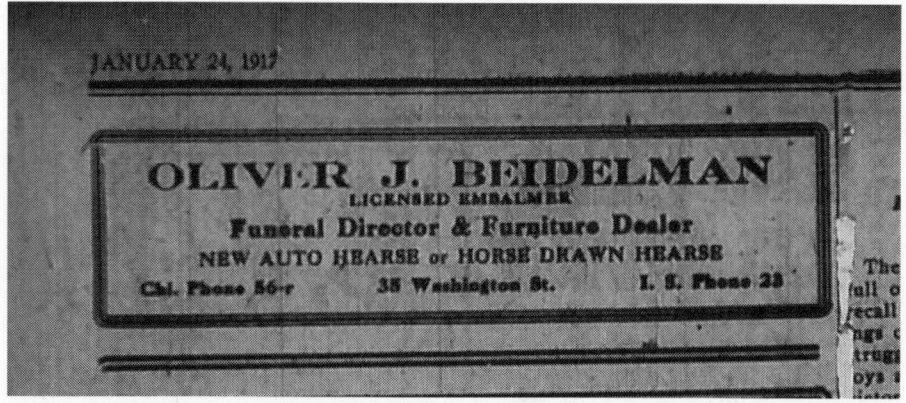

Beidelman Funeral Home ad, 1912

Home Sweet Home

Charles was never so happy to see Jessie as he was when she met him at the Helena train station. It felt so good to put his arms around Jessie, and put Naperville - and its foolishness - behind him for good. In the days that followed he shared the story of Harvey's banana potion with Jessie and, they too, had a good laugh at Harvey's expense.

With Dad gone, Mom wrote Charles more frequently, keeping him up to date on developments in Naperville. Namely, she had decided to take over William's role in the affairs of Hillegas Hardware; after all, she needed something to keep her mind off the misery of her loss. Harvey, now that dad was gone, has decided that he and his wife Jenette will move out west - he's got his eye on Los Angeles. Ida, Simon, and the grandchildren will keep Mom company for the holidays and such.

Knowing that Mom was content in Naperville was a big load off of Charles' conscious. It was a good town, good people too, they would look after her. Charles knew that he and Jessie couldn't go back to Naperville permanently, even for Mom - just too much baggage there.

The End of the Road

It had been five years since dad passed, and life for Charles and Jessie continued as a blessing. As they approached their 10-year anniversary, November 1st, 1911, they reveled in, each other, the happiness that they've shared, and the future of their love. They loved each other more today than they did on their wedding day - 10 years ago in that old Butte, Montana courthouse; the bond of their affections actually grew stronger with time. They knew now that nothing could ever separate them, *ever.*

A Promise Made

In April of 1912 Jessie began to grow ill. Day by day she was weaker and sicker. She felt so very sick. Then, on May 1st, 1912, Jessie Hillegas closed her eyes for the last time. Charles held tightly to her hands - they gradually grew cold in his grasp. At the tender age of just 36, ten years into her marriage to Charles, Jessie Robateene Massey-Hillegas slipped into eternity on a Spring day in the beautiful state of Montana.

The depth of Charles' sorrow was too deep for him to bear; his only reason to live was gone. He stared at her lifeless shell, praying that she'd awake - praying it was just a nightmare. He begged her to come back to him. "Please God, I will do anything to have her back. Please?" Jessie remained lifeless and still. Charles rambled to himself, "There must be a way to bring her back. There must be - " -Charles stopped in mid-sentence. His memory went back to his father's graveside, in the Naperville Cemetery, six years ago, to the conversation he had with his brother Harvey...

"The potion brought back life..."

"I know the chicken was dead, I'm positive. But, somehow, it was alive again..."

"All our elixirs were garbage, except one... I tweaked it, and it brings back the dead."

"Do you remember your banana potion..."

"I now it sounds crazy, but it worked - it brings back the dead..."

Charles' mind was reeling: '*What if Harvey was right? What if the formula that he concocted does bring the dead back to life?*' Charles began pacing the floor frantically, asking himself out loud, "How can I bury Jessie without knowing for sure if the potion would bring her back? I can't bury her until I know. I have to know. I must try the potion on Jessie. Jessie, I promise you, I will try..."

Charles turned and looked in the dresser mirror, his eyes were red and bloodshot from crying, his mouth uncontrollably quivering from heartbreak and hopelessness. He stared into the reflection of his own eyes. He reached his hand up to the mirror, and, touching his hand's reflection, he stared intently into his own eyes as he spoke to himself in the mirror. "I will bring her back... I will bring her back... I can do this... " Then he turned to Jessie, lying lifeless on the bed, he said, "In my mother's house are my notes. In the notes may be your life. Harvey was probably wrong, but we have to try. I have to find those notes to discover how Harvey tweaked my formula."

Charles walked out into the hallway of the boardinghouse. There he lifted the telephone earpiece from its resting place. He put the receiver to his ear and spoke into the mouthpiece, "Ahoy, operator? Can you connect me to the town of Naperville? It's in Illinois. Yes, number 361. Please hurry."

Telephone, 1912

After a moment someone picked up the line, Charles responded, "Hello, Mother? Charles. Not so good mom. I've lost Jessie. Just a few minutes ago. No, she's been very sick for a while. I'd like to bring her to Naperville, to our family plot, with your permission. Thank you. We'll leave right away." Charles hung up the phone. He went back to their room and sat down on the bed next to Jessie. He lovingly brushed her hair from her face. Then he leaned over and whispered in her ear, "Jess, *we're going home.*"

Sunday, May 5th, 1912

The three-day journey from Montana seemed like a million years. Charles kept telling himself that soon they would be back in Montana, he and Jessie happy again, together. All he has to do is get her to Naperville, find the notes, mix Harvey's banana concoction, feed it to Jessie, and then...

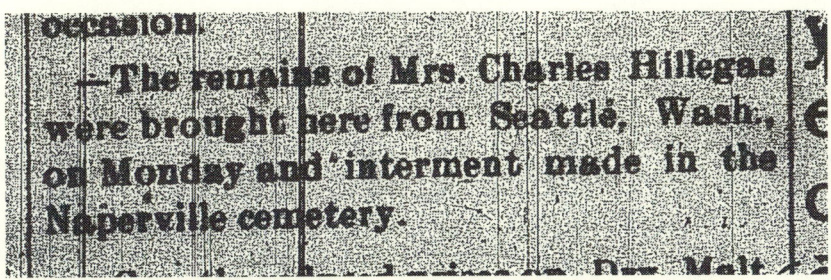

Snippet from newspaper May 6, 1912

The sun was setting behind him as Charles noticed the Naperville depot growing larger out his window; the journey from Montana to Naperville was almost over.

As he disembarked the train, representatives of Beidelman's Undertaking establishment of Naperville met Charles. They carefully removed the casket from the train and loaded it into their motor hearse for the short transport to the location of tomorrow's funeral service, the home of Charles' mother.

Mary met her heartbroken son Charles at the front door, as he entered, a cool spring breeze blew through the house. The casket was brought in right behind him and set up in the front parlor of house for the service. Seeing the casket in the front parlor of the house conjured memories of William's funeral service in the home just six years ago. Jessie's funeral service would begin tomorrow morning, 9am. Charles didn't have much time. He had to find his notes, mix the elixir, and feed it to Jessie, all before 9am tomorrow. He had a quick dinner with his mother and retired to his room.

The first thing to do was to find the notes. Charles tore his room apart looking for the notebook, no success. Harvey had it last - maybe it was in his room somewhere? Charles snuck into Harvey's old room, being extra quiet so as not to wake up mom. He began to rummage through Harvey's belongings - no success. Was it on Harvey's bookshelf? No. *Damn him, where could he have put it?* Charles searched the house late into the night without finding the notebook. *Maybe Harvey destroyed it? Maybe he'd brought it with him to California? Damn...*

It was early twilight when Charles gave up his search and went into the parlor. Jessie's casket lay in the dark, on a beautifully decorated table in the corner. He walked up to it and put his hand on it, sighing, "I have failed you. I'm sorry." He sat down on the sofa, pulled a small blanket over himself, and closed his weary eyes.

The next thing he knew his mother was next to him, jostling him from his slumber. She tapped him on the knee and whispered, "God bless you Charles, I pray that the good Lord gives you strength. There are few things on this earth as difficult as laying a loved one to rest. You're a good son." He put his arms around her to warm her up; the room was cool. After a moment, she stood up, already exasperated, and sighed, "Come now, we've a long day ahead of us..."

Monday, May 6, 1912

As Charles had expected, the funeral gathering was slight; he and Jessie weren't looked upon with much respect in Naperville. Still, Jessie received a better send off than she'd have gotten had Charles buried her in Montana. The Hillegas family burial plot was large, and located in a beautiful section of the Naperville Cemetery on Washington Street.

Charles wasn't sure that dad would have agreed to Jessie's inclusion in the family plot, but mom did, and hers was the only voice that mattered on this cool May morning. The minister said a few kind words in the parlor of the house as well as in the blustery morning breezes graveside. Jessie was laid to rest ten feet north of her father-in-law William in the Naperville Cemetery.

Following the service, Charles, his sister Ida, her husband Simon, and Mom, went back to the Hillegas house on Front Street. Charles went right up to his room to think about his future. *What to do now? Should he stay here in Naperville and help Mom with the store? Should he head back to Seattle, where he lived before marrying Jessie? How could he possibly carry on at all without her?* - So many things to sort out.

As Charles lay there on his bed, he began to think about his youth; so many lazy afternoons were spent laying on this bed thinking about mixing herbs and roots into new elixirs. Dad thought he and Harvey were crazy – maybe they were. They used to spend so much time in the barn mixing potions...
The barn?
Charles jumped to his feet. *The barn!*
He hadn't looked for the notebook in the barn!
He rushed down the stairs and out the back door, tripping over himself to get to the barn as fast as he could. When he got there, he threw a door open... - The afternoon light crept in, filling the darkness. Off to the side was a workbench, piled high with years of junk and dirt. Charles began to quickly clear away the debris.

It only took a few seconds. There it was: the notebook.

Charles grabbed it and ran out into the yard, for the sunlight. He frantically turned the pages looking for the mixture Harvey had talked about – something to do with banana...

He neared the end of the notebook without finding it, *damn, had Harvey removed it? Wait, there's one that looks interesting...* Charles tried to make out his faded writing. *This one claims that it cures weariness and increases energy – and the primary ingredient is banana. This is it! This is the one! This is the elixir Harvey was talking about. There are additional ingredients in the recipe that are written in Harvey's hand. There is writing on the page bottom from Harvey as well...*

It reads:

Using Chuck's energy elixir as a base, I adjusted the formula in the recipe as noted above. In my experiments with chicken incubation, I fed this new mixture to several of the chickens. I am stunned to submit here that something very peculiar happened.

It sounds unthinkable, even blasphemous, but this new mixture of mine appears to reanimate life in the lifeless.

Harvey Hillegas, 1906

Charles closed the notebook. He sat down in the grass. Time seemed to stand still as he contemplated his options. '*This is the mixture that could bring Jessie back to me. This is the mixture that can change everything. I've got it. But in order to try it, I'll have to steal Jess from her grave and bring her back here, to the barn...*'

The Impossible Plan

Charles went up to his room clutching the notebook under his arm. He laid on his bed thinking, '*If I'm going to do this, it has to be as soon as possible.*' He took a deep breath, leapt from his bed, and headed down to the kitchen to secure the ingredients for the elixir. Then, he returned to his bedroom and followed the "recipe" meticulously.

It only took a few moments to produce. He held it up to the light, as he whirled the mixture in the cup; it was yellow and thick, and smelled like bananas – certainly didn't look like it could work miracles. He then hid the cup of elixir from his mother's view by tucking it under his shirt as he made his way out to the barn.

He set the cup on a shelf and began looking around the barn for the equipment he'd need to get Jessie back to the barn. He secured a shovel, a lantern, and a two-wheeled cart. Confident in his success, he made a comfortable place in the hay for Jessie to lie down. Then, he went up to his bed to wait for an opportunity to slip away unnoticed.

Saturday, May 11, 1912

Five days had passed since Jessie's burial. Charles was going crazy with the stress of implementing his plan; he'd been waiting for a perfect time to slip away, but he couldn't put it off any longer. He resolved that tonight he would see it the plan through.

As the sun set and Naperville grew dark, Charles knew that his Mother would soon be retiring for the night. Soon, he heard her footsteps coming up the stairs; then they sounded as if they were coming toward his room. Then, a gentle wrap echoed on his door.

He said, "Yes?"

His Mother pushed the door open and peered in, "Goodnight Charles. It's difficult to believe, I know, but tomorrow will be a better day."

Charles nodded, "Thanks. Goodnight."

She turned and slowly made her way to her room and closed the door. Charles jumped up and quietly rushed outside to the barn.

The night was cold. Charles looked around to make sure none of the neighbors were outside - *he was alone*. He grabbed the shovel, lantern, and cart. As he headed out, he stopped to think which three-quarter-mile route to the cemetery would be best. *Ellsworth Avenue south to Chicago Avenue would be fine to get to the cemetery but the steepness of Fort Hill will be too difficult on the return trip, pushing the cart with Jessie in it. He could cut through Central Park to Washington Street, and take Washington down to the cemetery. That would be fine to get to the cemetery, but Washington Street is too busy to get Jessie back home without being noticed. The only way he could determine - the way that would provide him level streets and privacy - would be to cut through Central Park, go west on Van Buren Avenue to Main Street. Then take the quiet side street Main south to the cemetery. The reverse route would work too.* He was happy with that plan.

He ducked down as low as he could and began his three-quarter-mile trek to the Naperville Cemetery.

The cemetery was pitch dark. Charles lit his lantern to help him find his way to Jessie's grave. The ground at her grave was cold, but soft, loose, and freshly turned, as he sank the shovel into the dirt. With each shovel-full he made his way closer to her. He could almost hear her calling to him. His heartbeat was driving him to a frenzy. His breathing grew rapid and shallow. He kept telling himself, *"Keep going, keep going."*

Just then an angry voice came from the darkness, "Hey! What business have you here?"
Charles looked up from his macabre task.
There, a man - the cemetery sexton - stood in front of him. "Well, damned fool, what's your business?"
Charles was speechless, defenseless.
The man held up his lantern to illuminate the trespasser's face. He could see by the fear in Charles' eyes that he had been driven mad, insane even. Fearing for his own safety, the sexton quickly defused the confrontational aspect of the situation and said, "You'll need a permit to remove a body from its grave, maybe you should get one."
Charles jumped at the opportunity, "I'll return with that then."
They parted company without further trouble. Charles went home thinking that the situation was over; the sexton however wasn't about to let a possible grave robbing go unreported.

The sexton then quickly made his way to the home of Oliver Beidelman, a prominent Naperville undertaker. He informed Oliver Beidelman of the peculiar events that had transpired in the cemetery. Mr. Beidelman, being a Hillegas family friend, and wanting to spare them any more trouble, told the sexton, "Don't tell the sheriff about this, I'll take care of it myself." The sexton obliged.

The next day, Sunday, May 12, 1912, Beidelman paid a visit to Mrs. Hillegas, informing her of Charles' actions in the cemetery the previous evening. He told her that Charles is undoubtedly going mad with the stress of his loss. He is losing reason and must be watched closely. Mrs. Hillegas agreed.

When Charles' mother asked him later that day why he had done such a horrid thing, Charles - unable to tell her that his plan was to bring Jessie back from the dead - said, "I had a vision that she was still alive." Mrs. Hillegas assured him that Jessie - having been in her casket for over a week now - is most surely with the departed. Charles nodded in reluctant agreement. Mrs. Hillegas felt confident that Charles now understood the reality of his wife's passing. But, what she didn't realize is that he had every intention of succeeding in his secret objective – to bring Jessie back from the dead.

He just needs another chance...

Monday, May 13, 1912

Charles knew he had to devise a new plan, and quick. The only way he was going to get Jessie was to elude the sexton, but how? He was racking his brain for a solution so hard that exhaustion set in and all he wanted to do was sleep. And that's when it hit him - *the sexton has to eventually go to sleep tonight!* That was Charles' mistake last time - the sexton hadn't yet retired for the night. *'Tonight,'* Charles thought, *'tonight, I'll watch his light. When his room goes dark, Jessie will be mine.'*

Charles stayed in bed until he was sure all of Naperville was sound asleep. Then he slinked out to the barn and secured the equipment he'd had last time. This time though there was an added guarantee for success: a gun. This time, no one is going to stop him - No one. He slipped the gun in his belt and stealthy made his way to the cemetery. As he entered the cemetery grounds he hid behind a tree and glanced over to the sexton's quarters – the light was off. Surely he was asleep by now, it's past 11. As an added precaution, Charles won't light his lantern unless he absolutely needs to. He, then, quietly, stumbled, in the pitch dark, over to Jessie's grave.

He waited a few minutes for his vision to adjust to the extreme darkness in the center of the cemetery where Jessie's grave was. He knelt in the fresh dirt and whispered, "Don't be afraid Jess, it's just me." He grabbed the shovel and sank it in the dirt.

With every shovel-full the grave opened larger and Charles was a little closer to Jessie. This time, unlike a few days ago, Charles was being much more deliberate and careful; making sure he stayed hidden and quiet.

As the grave grew deeper it also grew darker near its bottom and Charles concluded that he had no choice but to light his lantern. He realized that doing so was to broadcast his presence to any passers-by, but there was no way he could continue so deep in the ground without light. He stuck a match and lit the lantern.

He placed the light at ground level, grabbed the shovel, and jumped back down into the empty earth. The lantern was doing its job; he could see that he didn't have that much further to go. It was than that he heard something, out in the dark. His heart skipped a beat, as he grabbed his gun. Was he caught again? *No one is stopping me, no one.* His finger tightened around the trigger. He stood still. He could hear people talking. It sounded like it was coming from Hillside Road. Maybe kids? He held perfectly still. The voices gradually began to fade off in the distance. Within a moment, they were gone and hadn't noticed him. He heaved a heavy sigh of relief as he looked at the gun in his hand – *he was losing control, this was driving him insane.*

With that close call Charles knew that he had to finish quickly, he took a deep breath and yet again thrust the shovel into the ground. But instead of the familiar sound of the blade piercing dank dirt, the hallow sound of wood echoed in Charles' ears. Realizing that he'd hit the top of the rough box that contained Jessie's casket, he stopped cold, threw the shovel down, and fell on his knees. He began to frantically sweep dirt away from the rough box lid. The damp dirt caked under his fingernails. He reached around to find the lid's edges and cleared the dirt away so he could get a grip on it. Then, bracing himself against the edges of the grave, he suspended his body over the box and gave the lid an adrenalin-induced yank. The wood cracked and creaked as the rough box lid surrendered its seal to Charles' determination. There, beneath him, lay Jessie's casket. He stepped onto the casket for stability, and maniacally ripped the rough box lid from its base. He tossed it up and out to ground level.

Charles was balancing himself over the casket, standing on the edges of the rough box. He reached down with his right hand and slowly pulled Jessie's casket open... The pungent and foul aroma of human putrefaction poured into the open grave. Charles began to cough, gasp, and gag. His eyes were watering. It was so dark. He felt dizzy. He reached for the lantern...

As the soft glow of the flame illuminated the interior of the grave, Jessie came into full view for Charles. She lay so still – as if sleeping. Her hands folded together on her stomach, fingers intertwined as if in prayer. He brought the lantern close to her, near her shoulders. Her once-beautiful face was sunken, drawn, and white. Her once-full lips were thin, blue, and cracked. The only remnant of her former beauty was her long brown hair;

even in this surreal moment her gorgeous brown main surrounded her peaceful face and fell gracefully down on her shoulders.

Charles didn't see the decay. Looking into the casket, he only saw his beautiful bride - as glorious to him as on their wedding day. A tear fell from Charles' face to Jessie's. How much he had been missing her...

He set the lantern up at ground level and took a deep breath of fresher air. He then stepped into the casket holding the lid open with his left leg. He bent over and unclasped Jessie's hands from each other. He wrapped her arms around his neck. He then slipped his hands under her shoulders and gently lifted her up from her casket. She seemed so cold and fragile. He lifted her higher as he slipped his left hand behind her, now cradling her in his arms. He paused for a moment and hugged her tightly, to warm her up, before raising her high and gently setting her out onto the ground level with a deep grunt.

Charles climbed out of the grave and sat on the ground beside Jessie - his heart was racing; he was nauseous, confused, and out of breath. He extinguished the lantern and - sitting in the dark - tried to gather his thoughts.

Exhausted, Charles reached for the two-wheeled cart he'd brought. He propped it upright next to Jessie. As he gently sat her in it, it was clear to him that it wasn't going to be practical - her arms and legs were hanging over the edges of the cart in a most "un-lady-like" way. Charles knew he didn't have the energy to carry her home either. He let out a frustrated sigh, "Damn." It was then that he noticed the rough box lid lying off to the side of the open grave. It gave him an idea.

He laid the lid over the top of the cart and then gently laid Jessie upon it, like a make shift stretcher. She looked much more "comfortable." He then moved the cart, with Jessie aboard, toward Hillside Road, to test it for stability. It seemed to be working. He grabbed his lantern and shovel and quickly began pushing the loaded cart across Hillside and north, down Main Street, en route back to his Mom's house, ¾ of a mile away.

As he made his way through Central Park, he could see, in a short distance ahead of him, his mother's barn. He felt great relief; he'd made it without getting caught.

Pulling the barn door open he went inside and lit the lantern. In the corner of the barn was the resting place he'd prepared for Jessie, it was a small pile of hay and looked satisfactory. He pulled the cart into the dimly lit barn stopping next to the small pile of hay. He then lifted Jessie from the rough box lid, and, while cradling her in his arms, he laid her down gently in the hay. Charles thought Jessie looked comfortable but he could see that the position of Jessie laying flat on her back wasn't going to work – in order to "feed" her, she'd need to be more propped up. Charles reached for the rough box lid. He stood it up behind Jessie with its top edge leaning against a barn support post. He then lifted Jessie into a partially standing position and leaned her against the lid. It worked.

Charles wiped the stress-induced sweat from his brow and reached for the cup that held the banana elixir...

Feeding Time

A faint ray of moonlight shone through the partially open barn door, the soft blue light fell softly across Jessie. Charles set the cup on the dirt floor as he knelt down next to her. He stared at her for a moment in disbelief - he couldn't believe she was here, in the barn - he had her all to himself. He looked down at the cup of potion, then back to Jessie's pale white face. Unsure how to proceed, he took a deep breath, gathered his nerve, and improvised the process: He cupped her face in his hands lovingly. Then, delicately he pushed his two thumbs into the corners of her mouth and pried her jaws apart. Her mouth fell open, almost invitingly.

Charles gulped, in surreal disbelief, this was it: the moment of truth. He whispered, "Whatever happens, I love you Jess, more than anything." He reached down and picked up the cup of potion, then he picked up a small nearby stick. He stirred the mixture in the cup with the stick for a moment and tossed the stick aside.

Holding the cup in his left hand, he reached over to the back of Jessie's head with his right hand. He grabbed her hair at the scalp and lovingly pulled it down to tip her head backward. Her mouth opened further, and her throat appeared wide. Charles put the cup edge to Jessie's lips and slowly poured the potion into Jessie's mouth. Her mouth filled quickly and the potion overflowed out onto Jessie's face. Charles stopped pouring to wait for the elixir the seep down her throat. After a moment her open mouth was drained of the potion and Charles again filled it with what remained in the cup. He waited a moment for her to "swallow" it all, and then, calmly, he pushed up on her lower jaw causing her mouth to close somewhat. He did it. It wasn't the neatest job - he'd spilled some of the potion on Jessie's face, neck, and dress. But that didn't concern him; the important thing is that Jessie drank most of it. He sighed, "It has to work. It has to... "

Charles kissed Jessie's forehead and snuggled up next to her to warm her up. He took one of her hands into his and he waited, all the while watching Jessie's hand very closely; waiting for it to twitch, move, or grab hold of his hand. Several minutes went by and her hand only seemed to grow colder. He pressed the back of her hand to his cheek and said, "You can do this

Jess. Come back to me. Come back Jess. Please come back. Please God. Bring her back."

As the hours passed, Charles felt the reality of failure sinking into his heart; with each moment he lost a little more hope.

Tuesday, May 14, 1912 – Early Morning

As the dawn of the new day was breaking, Charles was still holding out a small hope that Jessie would come back, that her eyelids would soon flutter, that she - in her soft voice, as if rising from a prolonged slumber - would very soon whisper his name. All his attention was focused intently on Jessie, watching for any sign of reanimation.

Just then Charles was startled as the barn door began to painfully creak as it slowly opened. Charles looked toward the door, realizing it to be his mother. She looked into the dark barn, straining to see in the limited light, "Charles are you in here?" She stepped in, "You weren't in your room, I thought maybe..." Her voice trailed off in shock as she saw Charles sitting in the hay. Beside him, Jessie - propped up, partially standing.

"Dear God..."

Charles was caught off guard. He grabbed his gun and pointed it at his mom. He wanted her out. *He needs more time. He couldn't give up on Jessie, not now. He just needs a little more time. Just a little more time.* He screamed, "Get out!"

In shocked disbelief she shook her head, unable to comprehend what she was seeing, "Charles? Charles, what have you done?"

His eyes grew wild and defensive. He stood up and aggressively approached her, all the while pointing the gun at her. "I said, get out! Now! Get out!"

She turned and ran to the door in terror, "I'm getting the sheriff..."

"Get out!"

Charles could hear her crying as she ran back to the house.

He looked down at the gun in his hand. He felt ashamed that he'd pointed it at his mother. He looked over to Jessie - nothing had changed. He felt his heart break. He heaved a heavy sigh, "It's over."

The Showdown

Within moments, Naperville's sheriff met Mrs. Hillegas in the front yard of her house. "Can you tell me again what is happening here, I didn't understand on the phone."
Mrs. Hillegas led the sheriff along the street and then pointed to her barn behind her house. "My son Charles recently lost his wife..."
The sheriff interrupted her, and shook his head in sympathy, saying, "I heard. Terrible thing. Terrible thing."
Mrs. Hillegas, frustrated, continued, "Yes. She died in Montana and Charles brought her back here to Naperville to be buried in our family plot in the Naperville Cemetery."
The sheriff nodded, "So I heard. She'll rest in peace there."
Mrs. Hillegas said, "Sheriff, he dug her up! They're in the barn! Both of them!"
The sheriff's eyes widened in disbelief, "The dead lady is in the barn?"
Mrs. Hillegas shook her head '*yes*'.
"God help us..."

The sheriff snapped into "sheriff mode" and quickly made his way to the barn while saying to Mrs. Hillegas, "Grave robbin' is against the law in these parts. Charley has done it this time." As he approached the barn he shouted to Charles, "Charley! It's the sheriff. I'll need you to come out of there, or I'm comin' in to get cha'." The sheriff waited a few seconds and then took a stance preparing to kick the door in.
Mrs. Hillegas grabbed his arm, warning, "He's got a gun!"
The sheriff turned to Mrs. Hillegas, "How do you know that?"
"When I saw them he was pointing it at me."
The sheriff backed away from the door. He rubbed the back of his neck to relieve the building tension, sighing, "That changes things. Don't want nobody killed over this."

By now neighbors began to gather around the area, curious about the commotion. They talked among themselves, saying, "I heard Mary tell the sheriff that Charley is in the barn with a gun." "Charley may be insane with grief, he lost his young wife last week, ya know."

The sheriff calmly rapped on the barn door to get Charles' attention, saying, "Charley, I don't want no more trouble here. I know what happened. Why don't you come out peacefully. I'll see that your wife is brought back to her grave all proper-like. What do ya say?"

There was no response from Charles.

The neighbors were in shock, asking, "His wife isn't in her grave?" "Where is she then?"

The sheriff asked again, "Charley? I need you to listen to me. You're in a heap of trouble and it's only gettin' worse. I need you to put down your gun and come out peacefully. Can you do that?"

There was no response from inside the barn. The sheriff was losing his patience. He motioned for Mrs. Hillegas to come near the barn door beside him. "Maybe you can talk some sense into him." Mary nodded in agreement.

She leaned in toward the door, "Charles? Son, I know you're scared. I know you're upset. I know how much you love Jessie. But she deserves to be at rest now. She can't find eternal peace in this old barn. We can help you if you'll let us. We can find a doctor for you. We can help Jessie by getting her out of this filthy barn and back to her resting place."

The gathering crowd let out a collective gasp. "Is his dead wife in the barn with him?" "That's what Mary said, I think." Several people, in shock, made the sign of the cross as they stood in horror at the macabre scene playing out before their eyes. "Dear God in heaven…"

Mary heard their gasps and murmuring. She turned toward them. She saw the vacant looks on their faces. Everyone involved was consumed with stunned disbelief. She had never known such shame, she turned back to the barn door, imploring her son, saying, "Charles, please, please end this nightmare. Please come out."

There was no response.

The sheriff motioned for Mary to join him, in the backyard, out of earshot of Charles and the growing group of spectators. "Look, the Hillegas family are pillars of our town, I know that, and I've tried to handle this as low key as possible to reduce the embarrassment of it for your family. But frankly, I'm afraid I have no choice but to bring in the county law enforcement. They ain't as understandin' as me. I'll give Charley another 40 minutes, till noon, to cooperate. If he ain't done so by then, he'll have to answer to the law of DuPage Country. I'm sorry Mary, but I got to keep the peace here, and frankly, I get nervous when an unstable man is unresponsive to the law, grave robbin', and waving a gun at his mother."

A tear rolled down Mary's cheek as she stared blankly forward and nodded in understanding.

The sheriff approached the barn door with new vigor and determination, shouting, "Charles? I need you to listen here. I've tried bein' patient with you, but it ain't workin'. Listen, grave robbing is a serious crime; you could see ten years of hoosegow for it. If you come out now, this whole mess can stay between the Hillegas' and the town, nobody else has to know about it. But, if I have to call in Sheriff Kuhn from Wheaton... Well boy, that's a new kettle of fish for you. We can do this easy-like, but I'll need you to come out. *Now.*"

There was no response.

The huge crowd now knew for sure that Charles had been grave robbing. They knew that he had lost his reason, dug up his wife, and was now hold-up in the barn with her remains. This level of horror was like nothing else that had ever occurred in their town.

The sheriff waited till noon, there was never any cooperation from Charles. He looked at Mary and sighed, "I'm sorry Mary. I'm callin DuPage." The sheriff returned to his office and notified the DuPage County Police, in Wheaton Illinois, of the situation. Within 30 minutes, DuPage County's Sheriff Kuhn arrived on the scene accompanied by City Marshal Ehinger and Deputy Sheriff Louis Graves.

As promise by Naperville's sheriff, the county police were no nonsense. They circled the barn and told Charles that if he didn't come out peacefully they were coming in for him. They waited a moment for him to cooperate. He didn't.

Sheriff Kuhn drew his gun and brazenly kicked the barn door open. He jump inside and quickly surveyed the interior for Charles. He wasn't visible. There wasn't anywhere to hide. Jessie stood, partially standing, in the hay pile. He called out, "Hillegas? Where are ya?" The barn was silent.
"Is he here?" Asked Deputy Graves as he entered the barn.
The sheriff continued peering into every corner of the barn, concluding, "Doesn't appear so."
Graves walked up to Jessie's remains. "Holy mother of God..."
Kuhn approached. "OK. He's not here. That means he's armed, insane, and out on the streets somewhere. You and Ehinger check the house, he may be hiding in there. Don't bring the mom - He's still got a gun and if he starts firing I don't want her shot. I'll stay here with his unfortunate wife, in case he comes back. And Graves..."
"Yeah?"
"Make it quick. If he's not in the house, we've got just six hours of daylight left to find him."
Graves nodded and left.

Kuhn turned his attention to Jessie. He stared at her with disbelief. He sighed, "What kind of man would do this? And why?" That's when he noticed that there was some type of foreign substance on Jessie's mouth, face, neck, and dress. He reached out and scooped some onto a finger. He checked its consistency by rolling it between the finger and his thumb - slimy. He sniffed it - it smelled like banana. He looked at Jessie in repulsed befuddlement, asking, "What in God's name happened here last night?"

Sheriff Kuhn stood up and went outside the barn. A large crowd of spectators waited for any news. Mary Hillegas sat alone in a chair in the backyard, staring at the grass. He sat down in a chair opposite her. "Can I ask you something?"

Mary nodded, but didn't look up at him.

"Do you have any idea why your son might have fed his wife bananas last night?"

Mary looked over to him in confusion, "I'm sorry...?"

Kuhn cleared his throat for a second, to buy time to rethink the question. "Your son's wife, what is her name?"

"Jessie."

Kuhn nodded. "Jessie? OK. Do you have any idea why your son might have fed Jessie bananas last night? There was banana in her mouth, on her face, even on her dress. Any idea at all?"

"Banana's?"

"Yeah. There's no mistaking the smell of them. Any idea?"

Mary's eyes grew wide as she remembered the way the townspeople, six years ago, laughed about Harvey's claim to bring back the dead with an elixir he had - an elixir made from bananas. Mary realized the horrid truth: Charles was trying to bring Jessie back from the dead last night... She put her hand over her mouth, a chill ran up her spine, tears welled up in her eyes, her lip quivered, her mind was numb.

Kuhn noticed the sheer panic on her face, he asked, "So you know why?"

Mary had no intention of sharing the banana elixir tale. She answered, "No. I have no idea. Bananas? That's absurd." She turned away.

Kuhn knew she was hiding something. "Well, if you think of anything, maybe you could contact me."

Mary didn't respond.

    Just then the two detectives came out of the house and into the backyard, Graves reported, "He's not in the house."

Kuhn looked to Mary, "Is there anywhere in particular you think he might have run off to?"

Mary just shook her head '*no*'.

Kuhn stood up and motioned for his detectives to follow him out to the street.

"We've got to find this guy. He couldn't have gotten too far, because, as far as we know, he's on foot. He probably left the barn right after the altercation with his mother this morning, so he's had a few hours head start."

Graves asked, "Where do we start?"

Kuhn nodded, "Well, he was born and raised here, so he knows the area like the back of his hand; if there's a place for him to hide, he knows where it is. Now, assuming that he stays on foot, he knows that if he goes south, west, or north, he'd be walking into farmland. That's a problem for him because he's no farmer. He won't fare well outdoors for long. If he heads east, toward Lisle, there's civilization. He'd be much more comfortable there. The easiest way to Lisle from here would be Chicago Avenue. We'll start there."

The detectives loaded into the car and headed east down Chicago Avenue toward Lisle. As they approached Dutter's Hill, about five miles east of downtown Naperville, they spotted a man, Charles' age, walking aimlessly along the road near an abandoned gravel pit. They pulled their car in front of him and exited.

As they approached him he said, "I knew when I saw the automobile that everything was up." Charles submitted quietly to his arrest. He was immediately taken to the jail in Wheaton, IL, the county seat for the town of Naperville.

Charles refused to give any explanation for his strange behavior.

Charles was arrested on suspicion of grave robbery, the penalty for which, if convicted, is one to ten years.

Epilogue

Charles Hillegas

Charles' signature as it appeared on court documents, 1918

Following his arrest, Charles was examined as to his sanity. The following Monday he appeared before Justice of the Peace O. E. Higgins on the charge of Grave Robbing. He was absolved of all wrongdoing. He spent a few months in a private Chicago hospital under observation before being released and taking up residence on Chicago's south side.

That week, the newspapers of the day (Naperville's Clarion & Wheaton's Illinoisian) called Charles "Grief Crazed" and a "Ghoul." But, in typical Naperville fashion, there were never any follow up stories on the arrest or Charles in general. As far as Naperville was concerned, even to this day, this event never happened.

In January of 1918, a few months following the death of his mother, Charles initiated a lawsuit in the DuPage Court. He was suing his brother Harvey, his sister Ida, as well as the men who purchased Hillegas Hardware, all renters in the commercial building, and the renter of the Hillegas house on Front Street.

According to the U.S. census, in 1920 Charles was living on the south side of Chicago. He is a Lodger and listed as widowed.

According to the U.S. census, In 1930 Charles was living in Naperville, widowed, and renting a boarding room on west Franklin Street, in Naperville. The building no longer exists.

This census for 1930 shows Charles living on Naperville on west Franklin Street

In 1940, Charles died, alone, at 72 years old, in a wretched DuPage County Senior Living Facility, in Wheaton Il, on September 7th. Funeral services were held at 2:30 pm, on a beautiful Monday afternoon, at the Oliver J. Beidelman funeral home, on Naperville's Washington Street. The Rev. George Kurn officiated.

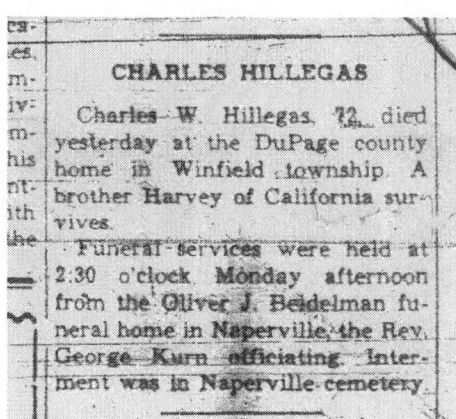

Charles resides in the Naperville Cemetery: Sec 3 Lot 944 Plot 11. Neither he nor Jessie have genuine tombstones, only cemetery markers. (See story: The Lost Graves)

Charles and Jessie never had children.

Jessie Hillegas

Jessie's remains were discovered to be unharmed when the authorities retrieved the body for reburial. However, folklore tells us that the Napervillians of the time quickly put two and two together and realized that the "Banana substance" found on Jessie was rumored to be the same life-giving Banana potion said to be housed at the Hillegas place. It was clear to everyone at the time that Charles dug up Jessie in an effort to bring her back to life.

Harvey & Jenette Hillegas

Harvey Hillegas had moved to California with his wife shortly after his father's death in 1906. He died at his home in Campo California on October 24th, 1943, after a short illness. His wife Jenette survived him. Although he had a place for burial here at the Hillegas family plot in the Naperville Cemetery, he chose to be interred in California. He resides in the Cypress View mausoleum in California.

Poor Harvey, his name was spelled wrong in his obituary. They spelled it Hilligas.

> **Summoned by Death**
>
> **HARVEY H. HILLIGAS**
>
> Word has been received from Mrs. Jinnie Hilligas of Campo, Calif., of the death of her husband, Harvey H. Hilligas, on Oct. 24 after a short illness.
> The funeral services were held from Merkally Austin parlors in Campo, Calif., on Oct. 28. Burial was in Cypress View mausoleum.
> Mr. Hilligas who was born in Naperville and spent most of his life here, had many friends who will mourn his passing.

Harvey and Jenette had no children.

Mrs. Hillegas (Maria, Mary)

Mary Hillegas tried to continue running the affairs of Hillegas Hardware but that effort only lasted for three months. The newspaper says that she has been running the business since her husband's death in 1906 – they make no mention of her two sons helping her. In August of 1912, a few months are the grave robbery, Mary Hillegas sold the Hillegas Hardware store to several men who had been in business with her husband; Charles sued them in 1918.

NEW HARDWARE COMPANY

The Hardware Business established many years ago by Mr. Wm. Hillegas and which, after his death, was carried on by his widow, Mrs. Wm. Hillegas, has been sold and is now being conducted under the name of the Hillegas Hardware Company.

This Company is composed of Mr. E. E. Sargent, President and Treasurer, Mr. Chas. A. Rassweiler, Vice President and Mr. C. H. Tobias, Secretary, who, together with Mr. H. H. Rassweiler and Mr. E. Mertz, constitute the Board of Directors. All these gentlemen are financially interested in the business. Mr. Chas. Rassweiler has been connected with this Business for the past nine years and Mr. E. Mertz for the past eighteen years.

It is the intention of the management to build up the stock of hardware and farm machinery and equipment so that all of their customers will find exactly what they want right in the store. In fact they propose to conduct a strictly up-to-date hardware and farm implement business. This will be accomplished as fast as the goods can be ordered and shipped in.

From August of 1912, just three months after the grave robbing

> —Mrs. Wm. Hillegas has gone to Los Angeles, Calif., where she will visit at the home of her son, Harvey Hillegas.

This appeared in the newspaper in October of 1912,
just five months after the grave robbing

Mary then moved to Los Angeles to visit her son Harvey. Once there, she decided to stay. She lived the last five years of her life in California, as far as she could get from Charles. She died at Harvey's house near San Diego California, at age 76, on January 4th, 1917. Her remains were returned to Naperville for interment at the Naperville Cemetery. Curiously, in life she ran away from Charles, but in death, she is buried right next to him. Her funeral was held on Friday, January 12th, 1917, at 2:30pm, at the First Evangelical Church of Naperville.

Ida (Hillegas) & Simon Schaefle

Charles' sister, Ida, died on March 5th, 1948, in Maywood Illinois. She was the last surviving member of the family. She and Simon had five children (Ada, Mary, Cora, John, & Corinne). There are no grandchildren, so the William Hillegas bloodline stops.

After the shame of the grave robbing, and the lawsuit in 1918, Ida had very little to do with her brother Charles, in fact she isn't mentioned as a surviving family member in his obituary. Sadly, Charles died alone, as a pauper, in a decrepit senior facility, while his sister and her family lived just 30 miles away.

In addition, as the last surviving member of the Hillegas family it was probably Ida who updated the family plot with the current proper tombstones. However, she did nothing with the graves of Charles and Jessie. It was as if they didn't exist at all.

Ida's husband Simon died in 1941. Ida and her husband Simon, as well as a few of their offspring, reside in the Naperville Cemetery: Sec 3 Lot 944.

And now the story with evidence and commentary portions inserted

The story of the grave robbing is in the Baskerville Font,

The evidence and commentary will be in the **Arial Font**.

It was a stifling day in Naperville, Illinois. William Hillegas, age 22, stood sweltering in the Zion church of Naperville on this, his wedding day – July 3rd, 1862. His beautiful bride, Maria Hartman, held his quivering hand as the ceremony began. William glanced back over his left shoulder, out into the pews – there, sat his parents-in-law, Adam and Susana, as well as his father, Joseph, all smiling back at him with pride. How he wished his mom could be here. '*Has it really been two years since the good Lord took her from us?*' he thought. He missed her more today than ever. She, too, would be so proud of him. He fought back a tear and turned to his bride. The look in his eyes told her what he was thinking; she squeezed his hand tighter in support for his loss. He felt better. He was in good hands.

William was born in Pottsville PA on August 4th, 1840. His bride Maria (Mary) Hartman was born in Lancaster PA on July 15th, 1840. Curiously, they were born the same year and their hometowns, Pottsville and Lancaster, are only 60 miles apart. One might wonder if they knew each other before moving to Naperville. Mary's obituary says that she moved to Illinois in her *childhood,* with her parents, and lived in the area all her life (except her final five years). According to William's obituary, the Hillegas Family moved to Naperville from Pennsylvania in 1857. William's mother passed away three years later, when he was about 20. William's father, Joseph, lived to be 90 years old and was a respected Naperville-area citizen and a devout Christian.

William's obituary (reprinted in the Appendix) tells us his wedding date and church affiliation. This wedding scene that I laid out here is as I feel it would have occurred - with all the in-laws in attendance and proud, William is of course missing his mother's presence but excited to begin a new life.

William and Maria immediately settled down in Naperville to begin their new life together. The years were filled with blessing. William's job at the Fridley Hardware Store in Naperville became a dream come true when he partnered with Louis Rieche and together they purchased the Fridley store on Jefferson Street. William was finally a business owner, a goal he'd long hoped and worked for. Then on August 3rd, 1863, William and Maria welcomed their first child; a beautiful daughter, they name her Ida May. When William's father saw the family growing he offered to buy a house for William and Maria as a wedding present. He could see that they were going to outgrow their current dwelling very soon. William accepted the kind offer, and the question became - where to build it?

William's early career, as portrayed here, comes from information outlined in his obituary. Below is an actual newspaper ad from January of 1870; it states that the Hillegas store is then located on Jefferson Street. Cemetery records are the source for Ida's birthday.

Let's discuss a completely misrepresented subject, the Hillegas homes:

First we'll clear up something that can be confusing in the discussion – the street names involved. In the history of the Hillegas homes, two street names are used: Front Street & Ellsworth Street. Note: *these are the same street*. Front is the original name of the street that was later renamed Ellsworth, after a prominent Naperville family named Ellsworth.

Second, there are two homes involved in the discussion. There is a purple/gray house on the southeast corner of Front Street and Benton Street; it is across the street from Sts. Peter and Paul church. Its address is 3 Front. The second house in question is also on Front Street, one block to the south of the first house, its address is 105 Front. It is a large three story red brick house. We will refer to these houses as "3 Front" and "105 Front."

Naperville folklore tells us that: *a Hillegas father bought a house for his son for a wedding present.* For many years, the common believe has been that William Hillegas bought the 105 Front house for his son Charles as a wedding present. This misinformation was probably started because a Naperville man named Pete Schrader misstated in a newspaper story, in 1973, that the house at 105 Front was built for Charles Hillegas as a wedding present. At the time he made that statement Schrader was 81-years-old. After that newspaper story, Naperville's Heritage Society, Historical Society, and more, accepted Pete's misinformation as true. Unfortunately, the misinformation continued to current time when Diane Ladley, too, published the misinformation as true in her Naperville book. She insisted that William Hillegas built the house at 105 Front for his son Charles as a wedding present.

Let's be clear: *it's not true.*

We know that a Hillegas father in all likelihood did buy a house for his son a wedding present. So the questions we need answers for are:

Which Hillegas bought the house?

Which Hillegas received the house as a gift?

And, where is it located?

Now, back in the "old days" there was talk in Naperville's folklore that the house at 3 Front was the house where the grave robbing occurred, and that it was in some way "connected" to the Hillegas family. What do we know about that house? We know the house was built in 1864. We know this because there is a plaque on it stating so (see image). I tried to get builder's records for the house with no luck. The county didn't have ownership records on the house going back to 1864. But, thanks to the plaque, at least we know when it was built.

Now let's look at the practical aspects of the commonly accepted folklore (that William Hillegas built the house at 105 Front for his son Charles as a wedding present.) Well, right out of the gate we've got a problem: *Charles was born in 1867 and the house at 105 Front was built in 1870.* Are we to believe that William built the house at 105 Front for his three-year-old son, as a future wedding present? I don't think so. Especially when we consider that when Charles sued the family in 1918 over the business affairs, he made no claim to the fact that the house was supposed to be his wedding gift and as such was rightfully his to take. He made no such claim. I think it's safe to conclude then that William did NOT build this house as a wedding gift for his three-year-old son. Also, when Charles married, in 1901, he didn't return to Naperville to claim his "gift house."

So, let's return to the house at 3 Front. What if this house was the one built as a wedding present for a son? Does the evidence support this idea? Actually, yes. Here's how: William was married on July 3rd, 1862; the house at 3 Front was built in 1864. We know that William's father, Joseph, was well off, and lived near by on a farm in south of Naperville. If Joseph told William and Maria on their wedding day that he was going to give them a house, it would take about 15 months to complete - that would be 1864! *The date on the house! I believe that Joseph Hillegas built the house at 3 Front and gave it to his son William as a wedding present.*

Also, William built the home at 105 Front in 1870, but, he was married eight years earlier in 1862 – where did he and Maria live all that time? I think the evidence supports the theory that they had been living at 3 Front. In addition, look at the proximity of the houses to each other. When William was building the home at 105 Front for his family, wouldn't it make sense to build it near where he was currently living, so he could more easily monitor the home's construction?

This theory matches up perfectly to all evidence. And, it solves the mystery.

The proud parents were very fond of Naperville's affluent east side. Which was fine, because, as a successful businessman in Naperville, that's where William and his family *belonged*. A modest and beautiful house was designed, complete with rising turret. They chose a plot of land across Benton Street from Sts. Peter and Paul Catholic Church, on the southeast corner of Benton and Front. They couldn't wait to move in.

This is the house built by Joseph Hillegas for his son, William, as a wedding gift.

That Damn Sense of Duty

Maria had fallen in love with William's strength. His character, she knew, was impeccable; his confidence, unshakable; his concern for others, honorable. He lived his life with a Christian drive to do the right thing regardless of personal cost. His life motto, printed on his heart, was: better to suffer wrong than do wrong. But she always knew, perhaps only in the back of her mind, that someday his sense of duty will be a sacrifice they'll all be asked to make. She knew it would happen *eventually* - she just didn't expect it to happen *so quickly*.

William Hillegas

As the Civil War raged on, the need for Union soldiers grew urgent. The plea for manpower soon reached Naperville and the heart of 24-year-old William Hillegas. Immediately his impulse was to help. Knowing that this decision could lead him to the ultimate sacrifice didn't discourage him at all; *it, after all, was his duty.* Surely, his wife and daughter will understand that. Maria was never more proud of him.

In 1864, William joined the war effort. He was a member of the Company D, 156th Illinois Infantry. He served until the close of the war, in Aril of 1865. He served bravely and received an Honorable Discharge. He returned to Naperville, his family, his business, and his new home.

This information on William's Civil War record came from his obituary.

And growing, and growing...

With the nation reeling from the assassination of President Lincoln, William continued to apply himself to growing his business, and growing his family. As 1866 gave way to 1867, the good news that Maria was again with child brought immeasurable joy to the Hillegas home. Maria, now being referred to as Mary, worked hard to be a devout Christian wife, neighbor, and mother, as she prepared for the second addition to the Hillegas clan.

This information on Mary comes from her obituary.

On July 25th, 1867, William's second child - a son - Charles William Hillegas, was born in that simple gray turreted wedding present. It didn't take long for William and Mary to realize that they needed more room for their growing crew, and besides, business was good. They agreed that a larger, more spacious, home is required. Something with high ceilings, comfortable rooms, farm area, perhaps a barn. *They will have the best house on Front Street.* Yes, this was a good idea. William went to work immediately.

Desiring to stay in Naperville's east side, they purchased a large piece of vacant land a block south of their current house, on the northwest corner of Front and Liberty Street. It had ample space for building; the east edge of the property ran along Front Street and continued all the way to the west, to Court Street. Public Square Park sat beautifully behind the property, just to the west.

The design was coming together; it looked like they'd be finished and moved in by early 1870. And just in time too – Mary is again with child, due in 1870.

When the house was completed it was beyond their dreams. It stood beautifully on the corner of Front and Liberty Street, a testament to the Hillegas success story. It was a stately three-story red brick building with a large veranda that bordered the front and side of the house. A large barn sat comfortably in the rear of the property, along Court Street. The interior of the home was as equally impressive as the exterior, boasting comforts that made it the epitome of 19th century living: 14 rooms, six chimneys, stove heating, as well as two parlors – separated by heavy double doors. In every way the house and grounds were stunningly beautiful. A large barn sat comfortably in the rear of the property along Court St.

The Hillegas house in the late 1800s. Note the barn in the rear of the property, on the left.

The Hillegas house then and now:

The details of the house come from a newspaper story in the Naperville Sun, Friday, May 11, 1979. The newspaper story is about the house receiving The Naperville Heritage Society Plaque and the society's acknowledgment of the home's historic significance to Naperville's history. Nowhere in the story do they mention the house's notorious past...

The property that the house sits on was originally plated as part of the "Sleight Addition." The Sleight's were one of Naperville's founding families and very instrumental in Naperville's early formation. It is believed, however, that a member of another influential Naperville family (by the name of Beidelman) owned the land at the time William Hillegas desired it. It appears that William Hillegas purchased the land from Beidelman.

There is also information that William, being a shrewd businessman, purchased not only the lot that his house was to sit on, but also a similar lot next to his, to the south. On this lot to the south, William built a house that was identical to his house; and he built it *at the same time he was building his house*! It was probably *very economical* to built two identical houses at the same time. Once the construction was finished, he sold off the "extra" house at a handsome profit. Today, the house that stood on the south lot no longer stands, but the story of its construction stands as a testament to the genius of William Hillegas.

Note: after World War II, housing in America changed forever - the suburbs blossomed. One of the reasons for suburban explosion was that builders in the suburbs discovered that they were able to greatly reduce the cost of home construction by building lots of virtually identical houses at the same time. For instance: They'd dig all the foundations at once, then pour all the concrete at once, then put up all the frames, then all the electrical, then the plumbing, etc., etc. It saved enormous amounts of time and money. – That "discovery" started in the late 1940s, but William Hillegas did it in 1870!

Naperville: Our Hometown

Once comfortably moved in, the Hillegas family took their rightful place among Naperville's influential. The Hillegas Hardware store continued to grow adding products such as: butcher knives, cooking & heating stoves, scales, spring buggies, food cutters, corn shellers, and bob sleighs. At this time Hillegas Hardware is also recognized as one of Naperville's most efficient and up-to-date offices. According to the ad, Hillegas Hardware did no business on Sundays.

This information comes from the following Hillegas Hardware newspaper ads and commentary.

Be sure to call

AT THE OLD

Farmers' Headquarters on Water St., Naperville,

before you place your order on any goods in our line. You will find the best assortment of

new up-to-date goods

in stock ever brought to this city. Will name a few:

Timothy, Clover and Garden Seeds, the old reliable Weber Wagons, Trucks and Milk Wagons; the old Schutler Wagons, Carriages, Buggies and Road Wagons—we have a new Buggy that needs oiling but once in six months—Deering Binders, Mowers and Corn Harvesters; Bardly X-Ray Sulky and Gang Plows; Rock Island Sulky and Gang Plows and Hay Loaders; the Defiance Sulky and Gang Plows and Bodlong Disc Harrows; Steel Harrows, 2, 3 and 4 sections; Walking Plows; Seeders, 6, 7, 8½ and 11 ft., with or without shovel; Wind Mills and Steel or Wood Tow and Pumps; Morgan Spading Harrows, Grinders, Corn Shellers; the White Sewing Machine; Sterling and Western Washing Machines, Wringers, Tubs, Cloth Baskets, etc.

Buy your Nails and Barb Wire now. Everything is going up in price.

We're on hand for business from 7:00 a. m. Monday to 9:00 p. m. Saturday of each week. Be sure to let us rest on Sunday. We want no one to call on us on that day for business of any kind.

W. H. HILLEGAS.

Through the 1800s, Naperville itself was growing as gravel roads were being extended in all directions. As well, Naperville was becoming a booming business center, adding among its offerings: Milling, Farm Machinery Manufacture, Buggy Making, Blacksmithing, Breweries, Hospitality, Furniture Manufacturing, Undertaking, Saddle Making, Tailoring, Winemaking, Cigar Manufacturing, Livery and Stables, Doctors, Surgeons, Quarrying, Dentists, Toy Factory, Photographers, Movie Shows, and Fine Dining. Stores opened to service the town, selling: Insurance, Jewelry, Books, Shoes, Drugs, Music Machines, Hunting Supplies, Oysters, Produce, Meat, and Gifts. There was even an American Indian who opened a storefront shooting gallery on Main Street.

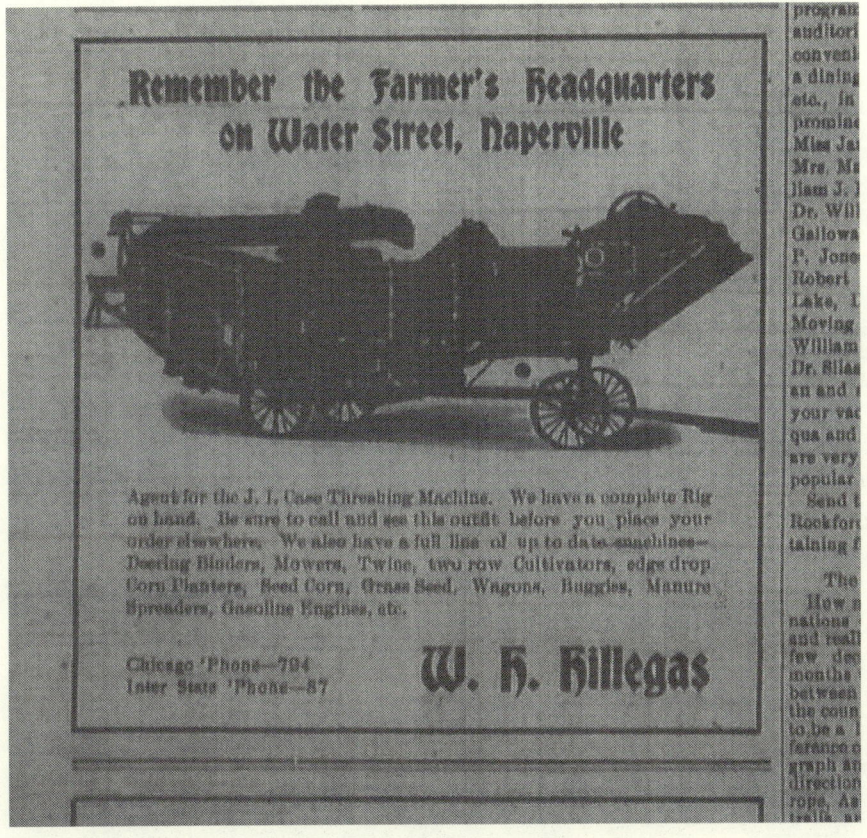

Hillegas Hardware ad - 1904

There was new business and opportunity everywhere. And of course, the perennial polar opposites were everywhere too: Churches and Saloons. Both were going gangbusters. Curiously, in the newspapers of the day, ads for saloons read: **All Welcome**. Ads for churches read: **Citizens Welcome**. **Strangers** *Generally* **Welcome**. Some things never change...

The list of Naperville businesses is compiled from actual ads that ran in the newspapers of the day.

The river that ran through Naperville was quite a bit different at that time than it is today. Namely, it was much wider; was known to have rattlesnakes; and, in the mid 1880s, was infested with Mink. They were causing major headaches, especially for the chicken farmers - Mink do like chicken evidentially. Many dealers were paying handsomely for the skins of the rascals.

This information on the "wily mink" was from a story in the Naperville Clarion newspaper, in August of 1886.

It was in this atmosphere that William was raising his family: a daughter and two sons. Home life for the Hillegas family was happy overall. William raised his family with devout Christian principals. Mary was a kind and caring mother, wife, friend, and neighbor. She was led to Christ in her early youth and lived her life with a strong personality, sterling character, and Christ-likeness. She filled her life with ministries of love and kindness; she even provided a couple of her favorite recipes to the locally produced hometown cookbooks.

Mary's obituary provided much of the information on her character mentioned here. Her cookie recipe from a Naperville Housewives Cookbook is also below.

> **THE NAPERVILLE COOK BOOK.** 47
>
> **SNOW CAKE.**
>
> One cup sugar, one-half cup butter, one-half cup sweet milk, two cups flour, whites of four eggs, two teaspoons baking powder.   Mrs. W. H. Hillegas.

William and Mary's eldest child, daughter Ida, grew up with the values of the time for a young lady - she married young to a local boy, Simon Schaefle, and began raising her own family. Harvey, the youngest, showed early the same drive for success that his father had. He endeavored to learn the ropes of business from his father by helping out in the new, larger, Hillegas Hardware store on Water Street. He joined the Naperville Hook and Ladder (similar to a fire department). And, at the age of just 15, would travel to Chicago everyday for lessons in Architecture, his hope to one day be an architect.

According to the DuPage County Marriage Records, Ida was married on May 24th, 1883, at 20 years old. Curiously, her husband's name is spelled differently in those records - they add an extra "e" – Schaefele.

Unlike Charles, Harvey was photographed working in dad's store, as well as volunteering with Naperville's Hook & Ladder Society (basically a fire department). The newspaper snippet below mentions Harvey's treks to Chicago to learn architecture.

> —Harvey Hillegas makes daily trips to Chicago for the purpose of becoming a first-class architect in the course of time. He is taking lessons from one of the leading artists of the city, and is making satisfactory progress in his studies.

This story appeared in the newspaper 1885

William's middle child, and eldest son, Charles, had an independent streak. He wasn't so much interested in following dear old dad's footsteps in the hardware business. But, the local drug store with its endless array of miracle potions and elixirs enchanted him. He was an intelligent lad, and enjoyed teaming up with his brother Harvey in the mixing of herbs and roots into new concoctions. A bout with pneumonia, in February of 1886, only strengthened his resolve to break new ground in this intriguing arena called apothecary. Charles was out of Naperville, away at school, for his early teen years.

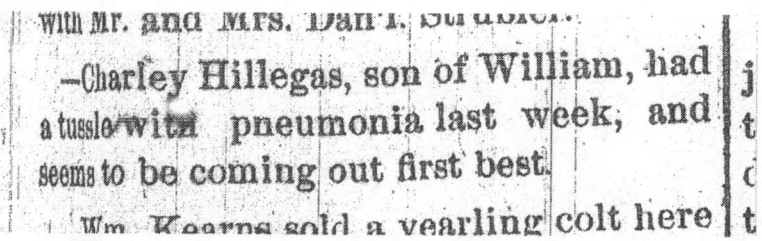

Charles was ill in February of 1886

Because there are several pieces of printed information concerning Harvey's various interests, and nothing about Charles (accept a mention in the paper about his tussle with pneumonia), Chuck and I have concluded that Charles was a typical middle child who an independent streak and kept to himself. The U.S. Census 1880 lists Charles as "At School." Since this is a census report, we can presume this means "away at school." - Charles would have been 13 years old. He could have been away at school for several reasons, the most likely ones being that he was either very smart, or very bad. Since the Wheaton newspaper, reporting on the grave robbing, comments that Charles "is highly educated," I will assume he's away at school because he's a very intelligent kid. Probably, in his mind, too smart for a "hick town" like Naperville! Which might explain why he's not interested in dad's small time hardware business or other pursues in small time Naperville.

The 1880 census showing Charles "at school"

Folklore tells us that Charles was into mixing herbs and roots into new elixirs and that he had a "potion" that he believed brought dead chickens back to life on the Hillegas farm. This presents a problem though, because, if Charles knew how to create such a potion, why didn't he mix it and use it when Jessie died in Montana? We believe that the potion was actually Harvey's mixture. This is why, when Jessie died in Montana, Charles had to bring her all the way to Naperville – so he could find the recipe for the formula that Harvey had created.

Dawn of a New Century

As America prepared for the changing of the century the Hillegas family continued to apply themselves to their business and family-related goals. Always striving to be at the forefront, Hillegas Hardware was one of Naperville's most efficient and progressive businesses. Hillegas Hardware was one of just 20 Naperville businesses to have telephone service in the early 1900s.

> ing freight, and he seems to enjoy the rush.
> —Hillegas & Co. have of one the nicest and neatest looking business office in town.
> —Dandelion "greens" are now served at dinner in all families that are up with the

A newspaper snippet from 1886

Curious with the William Hillegas family are the noticeably absent photographs of them. Try as we might, we could find no personal photos of the Hillegas family. Even Mrs. Hillegas' obituary in the Naperville Clarion contains no photo. The only photos of the Hillegas family that we could locate were photos taken for "Official" purposes. For instance, the photo of William on this page was taken in 1876 when William was elected trustee of the village board. The photos of Harvey Hillegas, in this book, were taken by newspaper photographers - one from the inside of the Hillegas store, and the other, is a photo of the Hook & Ladder Society, of which Harvey was a member. We had hoped for a photo of Charles in his arrest record, but alas, *there was no arrest record*. As far as I can tell, there are no photos of Charles Hillegas other than a spectacular photo of his ghost captured by a participant of my tour back in 2011. I do show the photo of Charles' ghost on the tour (no, it's not an orb!)

The absence of Hillegas family photos couldn't have been due to financial limitation, as the Hillegas family was doing well in that respect. It also couldn't be "opportunity" because there were a couple very respected photographers in Naperville's ranks of businesses in the late 1800s. Therefore, it may have been one of these three reasons: William simply placed no value on photography, or that he perhaps had a superstitious belief regarding being photographed, or it could be that William was just too cheap to pay photography fees. Whatever the reasons, it's a shame.

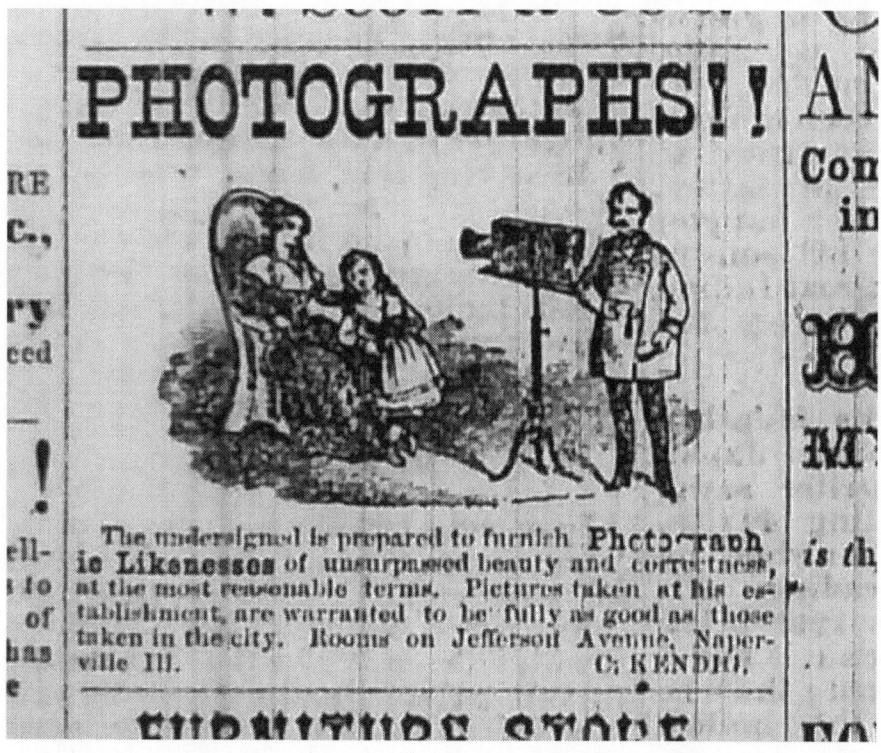

Christian Kendig was a popular Naperville Photographer.
This ad is from 1870

Then, in 1899, Harvey Hillegas married a beautiful young lady named Jenette (her friends call her Jinnie). In attendance at the wedding was a Hillegas-family friend, a young lady that Charles had been smitten-with for a long time, her name was Jessie - Jessie Robateene Massey. She lived in nearby Will County and was married to an angry and abusive husband, George F. Scollard. Jessie had been born in England in 1876 and came to America with her family when she was just a young girl. One of the first things her parents did when they arrived here was to marry off their 15-year-old flower, Jessie. The marriage was on December 11, 1891. The man they chose made life unbearable for Jessie, an abusive hillbilly. It broke Charles' heart every time he'd talk to her about it. Her eyes were so sad; how he wished he could help her. If only they had married her off to Charles, she'd be treated like a Queen...

According to English records, in 1876, Manchester England, Jessie Robateene Massey was born to Robert Massey and Marie Ellen Massey. In addition, her marriage license to Charles states that Jessie was born in Manchester England.

On the day of Harvey's wedding, Charles saw Jessie enter the house and immediately approached her. As he spoke to her he realized that there was something different about her - her smile seemed more natural, her adorable English accent seemed more... upbeat. He didn't have to ask her why, she offered it - "I'm going to leave George. I can't take it anymore. Eight years with that pig is enough. I know it's horrible, but I'm going to get a divorce from him. I've never felt so alive. He doesn't know yet. I'm afraid of him so I'm going to run away and stay with friends in Indianapolis till it's over." Charles saw this situation as his chance; Jessie could now be *his wife*. He didn't say anything to her then, but his mind immediately began making plans...

George F Scollard and Jessie R Massey

First Name:	George
Middle Name:	F
Last Name:	Scollard
Gender:	Male
Spouse First Name:	Jessie
Spouse Middle Name:	R
Spouse Last Name:	Massey
Spouse Gender:	Female
Marriage Date:	Dec 11, 1891
Marriage Location:	Will, IL Map
Record Type:	Marriage Record
Collection:	Illinois Marriage Records
Certificate:	Hard Copy Certificate

The Will County Marriage records gave us the information concerning her first marriage to George.

There are no solid historical leads that prove Jessie communicated her displeasure with her marriage to Charles at Harvey's wedding. I feel though that given the other evidence, it made sense that it occurred this way. The logic is as follows:

Charles and Jessie were married, in Butte Montana (near Helena), in 1901. Yet, just one year prior to the marriage, in the 1900 U.S. Census, Charles is living in Seattle Washington - alone. He is single, living in a boarding house - no mention of Jessie in the census. So, she isn't there with him.

Charles' and Jessie marriage license 1901, Montana.
Thank you to Brian Ogg at the Naperville Historical Society
for helping us secure this document.
The license is reprinted in larger format in the Appendix.

When they get married a year after the census, in 1901, the marriage license lists her current residence as Indianapolis Indiana.

Here's the problem: In 1900, Charles is in Washington while Jessie is in Indiana. Yet, in 1901 they are getting married - when did they fall in love? They were 2200 miles from each other!

I believe they were already in love, before Charles left for Seattle. I believe Jessie lived near by Charles when he lived in Naperville – this because she was married and living just a few miles from Charles, in Will County – back in 1900, that could be as close to Charles as a few miles.

So what could have sent Charles out to Seattle in 1900? I feel that his brother's wedding is 1899 is where Charles' plan to court Jessie began. I believe Jessie was also in attendance at the wedding. I believe this is where Charles found out that Jessie was planning to leave her husband. I believe Charles presented, to his parents, his plans to "rescue" Jessie and they – being devout Christians and believing wholeheartedly that divorced people are adulterers – forbade Charles from continuing any further love interest in Jessie. This caused him to conclude that the only way to have Jessie was to move away from Naperville and his parents. He chose Seattle. If he left Naperville right after Harvey's wedding, he would have been in Seattle – single – for the 1900 census.

Jessie probably lived in Will County during her marriage to George, but fled to Indiana during the divorce. This because: if she had lived in Indiana with George during her marriage to him, she probably would not have made the trek to all the way to Naperville (200 miles) for Harvey's wedding. Also, if she lived in Indiana during her marriage, she'd have been 200 miles from Charles – how did their love blossom? I believe she lived near to Naperville during her marriage to George, but moved to Indiana during the divorce.

Jessie lived in a time when divorce was basically not an option. Marriage was forever, come hell or high water. A woman stayed married no matter what. Not only that, the Bible taught that divorce was not acceptable to God, except in cases of adultery. The problem was, divorce wasn't "socially acceptable" no matter what the reason. Jessie was going to be branded a sinner and adulterer for the rest of her life. And she was only 23! Yet, she was going to get the divorce anyway.

I believe that Jessie's husband George abused her. I believe Charles loved Jessie and wanted to take her away from him. I believe Harvey's wedding was the place that Jessie told Charles that she was going to change her life, and Charles decided to make Jessie his wife.

The Line in the Sand

In the days that followed, Charles realized that the first step in making Jessie his wife was to secure the support of mom and dad. He sat down with them in the parlor. He explained the situation, and asked for their blessing. To his surprise, he was met with complete rejection. William erupted, "Absolutely not! Marrying a divorced woman will make you an adulterer - the Bible is clear on this fact. It is her duty to remain with her husband. Her actions are shameful and will under no circumstances be tolerated in the Hillegas home. She is partnering with the devil and Charles shall have no part of it." William stormed out of the house.

Mary remained at the table and wept. Charles went upstairs to his room. He counted out some cash he'd tucked away. He packed a bag and made his way to the train station.

Given what we know about William's Christian beliefs, and his strong personal ethic, it is pretty clear that William would want no part of a woman like Jessie. The thought that she would marry his son, perhaps bear his grandchildren, probably would have driven him to unparalleled fury. Disowning Charles was the only option William had.

Charles had to choose between having his parents, brother and sister, or Jessie. He chose Jessie.

It seemed like forever waiting for a train, but soon a light was faintly visible down the tracks to the east. He didn't care where it was destined; he just wanted to get as far from Naperville as he could. As he boarded he asked the conductor how far he could go with the money he had. The conductor counted it out and told him that the train goes all the way to Seattle Washington, and Charles had enough to get there. Charles handed the money over and plopped down in the seat. He watched out the window as Naperville grew more distant, he angrily sighed, "Damn hillbilly dump."

Westward Ho

Charles didn't have a specific destination in mind. He and his brother had often talked about living in the west; Harvey was targeting Los Angeles. Charles didn't have a preference and at this point anyplace that wasn't Naperville would suffice. Charles was a few days into his exodus, when he heard the conductor call out that the next stop was Helena Montana. Charles had heard of that place, lots of silver prospecting going on as he recalled. He decided to disembark there.

Charles set his bag down on the Helena Depot platform, and stretched; it had been a long time just sittin'. It was clear that this was a busy place, not the quiet hovel that Naperville was. He sought lodging and settled down for a good night's sleep.

As the days passed Charles realized that if you weren't a silver miner or John this just wasn't the place to settle down. It was a progressive city though, that's for sure; every convenience and pleasure was to be had. It wasn't for him; he decided to continue his travels on through to Seattle.

Helena at the time was part of the west coast gold/silver rush. Many people were strutting back into town with newfound wealth in golden hue. Of course, where there's cash there's a red light district, and Helena had a big one. It is for this reason that I believe Charles continued on to Seattle, in short order. We know Charles was intelligent, and ultimately a romantic, so perhaps gold diggers and whores just weren't his style.

Making a New Home

Seattle was much more to Charles' tastes. It was big and beautiful, full of opportunity and friendly people, and the ocean... Charles had never seen anything else like it. He loved it. Yes, Seattle would do nicely, and besides, he couldn't get much further from Naperville if he tried. One of Charles' first orders of business was to get in touch with Jessie. She didn't know that he had left Naperville and was now living practically in the Pacific Ocean.

Charles would take odd jobs to pay the bills, all the while keeping an eye on the post - waiting for a letter from Indianapolis. It had been months since he'd written to Jessie. He explained to her what had happened with his parents. He explained how he didn't care what they or their Bible thought of him. He loved her more than anything, and he wanted her to come be with him forever. He hoped that she felt the same way. He waited for a response. And he waited.

With each passing day the tight feeling in his chest would grow more uncomfortable with the realization that maybe he'd made a mistake. Doubts began to set in; maybe she didn't love or want him. He looked out the boarding house window, a fall breeze was blowing the multicolored leaves along the ground; he wondered if she'd ever really be his.

Between Harvey's wedding in 1899, and Charles wedding in 1901, about two years passed. So the question is: what was happening between Charles and Jessie during that time? We know that Charles moved to Seattle, alone (census data), and yet somehow during that time communicated with Jessie in Indiana (we know she was in Indiana because when she marries Charles in 1901 she lists it as her current residence). I lay out in this section my opinion how Charles and Jessie filled those two years, and how they ultimately ended up married.

1900

With the new century Charles was still hopeful for a life with Jessie. He'd sent several letters over the last year without a response from her.

Then it happened.

Tucked away in his daily mail was a tattered envelope. He didn't give it much notice until he spotted the return address city: Indianapolis Indiana. He threw the other letters on the desk and sat on the edge of his bed near the window. He looked at the outside of the envelope, thinking, 'so that's what her handwriting looks like..." He gently ran his fingertips over the ink for a few seconds.

He flipped it over and ripped the envelope open. He removed a letter, folded in thirds. He eagerly unfolded it, his eyes quickly scrolled to the bottom, and his heart skipped a beat. It was there - she'd signed the letter: Love, Jessie.

With renewed enthusiasm he read the letter in full. She apologized for taking so long to write. But, she explained, the divorce process had been much more difficult than she anticipated; her husband had been much more resistant than she anticipated; her family much less supportive than she had anticipated - the last year had been a nightmare. The only peace she got came from Charles' letters. They were the light at the end of her tunnel. Charles was the only person who understood, the only person not condemning her. She knew in her heart that they belonged together. But, she asked, "how?" They were now a million miles from each other.

Charles quickly wrote back to her with a plan: he was coming to get her, and bring her back to Seattle. Here they could start over, both of them, together...

Because the cost of using a telephone was extremely high, I believe Charles and Jessie would have communicated by mail. I also believe that Jessie would have met quite a bit of opposition in her decision to divorce George – not only from George but her family as

well. There was probably very little, if any, support for her in her decision. The fact that Charles was willing to throw away everything in his hope to win her may have been the only light at the end of her tunnel, and the primary reason she fell in love with him.

A New Life Begins

In late October 1901, Charles arrived in Indiana to meet Jessie. They immediately boarded a westbound train to take them back to Seattle to get married. On the way, they discussed their life together. Charles' heart would beat faster just hearing Jessie speak; her eyes would twinkle when she gazed at him. They couldn't wait to be man and wife.

Charles suggested that they not wait until Seattle to get married; he knew of a city where they could get married, honeymoon, and celebrate their new life. The city, he said, was near Helena, Montana; it was called Butte. In was in Silver Bow County. Jessie smiled and threw her arms around him.

On Friday, November 1st, 1901, the train pulled into the Helena depot. Charles and Jessie disembarked and headed for the courthouse building for a license and a quick wedding ceremony. Charles is 34, Jessie 23.

The courthouse in Silver Bow, in 1901

But, before she allows him to say, "I do," there is something very important she needs Charles to know about her...

Jessie led Charles to a bench in the courthouse entryway. They sat down, close to each other. She started to cry. "I should have told you earlier, I'm so sorry."

Charles' heart was breaking as he concluded that she didn't love him after all.

Jessie sniffled, and rubbed a tear from her eye, "We can't get married, I'm sorry..."

Charles felt like the his world was ending, "Why? I love you Jess. I love you..."

Jessie nodded as if she understood, saying, "I'm still married to George."

Charles pushed back, perplexed, "I thought.... I thought... the divorce?"

"It never happened. I tried! But without help... I couldn't do it alone. It was so hard. I tried... I wanted to tell you before..."

Charles took Jessie's hand and kissed it. "Do you still love George?"

"God, no."

"And you love me?"

"More than anything."

Charles smiled. "Then we belong together. Divorced or not, Jessie will you still marry me?"

Jessie laughed, "I don't think they'll let us do that!"

"When we go in for the license, just tell them that you are divorced, they'll believe you."

"You'll be marrying a married woman."

Charles chuckled, "Dad practically sold me for fertilizer for marrying a divorced woman, I wonder what he'd say about a married woman?"

Jessie kissed Charles, and whispered in his ear, "I'm divorced in my heart..."

We know that Charles, according to census data, is in Seattle, single, in 1900. But by October of 1901, he is marrying Jessie. This is proven by their marriage license, shown below. I believe they chose Butte to get married because Charles had spent some time there on his previous trip from Naperville to Seattle and thought it was as good a place as any.

[Marriage License from The State of Montana, County of Silver Bow]

The exchange between Charles and Jessie on the bench, concerning her divorce, is based on

something that Chuck and I had assumed to be true all along – Jessie never legally divorced George. The reason we felt that way was because we could find no divorce record for Jessie anywhere. There was proof of Jessie's marriage to George, but not a divorce from him.

In reality, this situation must have played out either of two ways:

1) Jessie didn't tell Charles that she is still married to George.

2) Jessie tells him that she's still married to George, and they work out a solution.

We don't really know which way Jessie chose to go. For this book, I opted for her being honest with Charles, and Charles taking the lead to do things his own way. I believe their love was very real, and indeed, continues beyond the grave. That's doesn't sound like a love built on Jessie deceiving Charles right out of the gate; it sounds like a love that no matter what trials it has to face, it will survive.

After the ceremony Charles and Jessie began celebrating in Helena. Jessie found herself growing fond of the place; it was exciting and vibrant. She had been cooped up in small towns for too long. She asked Charles if he wouldn't mind staying in Helena for a while. What was the hurry to get to Seattle? Charles wasn't fond of Helena, but he'd do anything for Jessie. They found a boarding room and settled down, *for a few years anyway*, Charles thought.

We know that Charles wasn't interested in living in Helena, as he didn't stay there for long on his previous trip – apparently just long enough to acquaint himself him it. We can assume that Jessie was the one who wanted to stay in Helena after getting married because Charles, when traveling alone two years earlier, didn't stay in Helena for long but continued on to Seattle.

We know that Charles and Jessie were living in Helena Montana, or an area around it, for a while after their wedding because there is snippet in a Helena newspaper about Charles suing the local bank for $213 that he feels they owe him. The newspaper snippet is dated March 16, 1902; it is reprinted below.

We had quite a bit of trouble ascertaining how long after the 1902 lawsuit Charles and Jessie remained in Montana. When Jessie died, the Naperville newspaper clipping (shown below) claims that her remains are coming from Seattle. So that suggests that sometime between 1902 and 1912 they moved to Seattle.

The question is: when did he and Jessie leave Montana to live in Seattle?

Answer: They never left Montana. That's why we can't find any evidence that suggests that they did.

What about the newspaper snippet that says Jessie's remains are coming to Naperville from Seattle? Most likely, it was the Seattle/Chicago train, and was simply referred to as "the train from Seattle."

For the next few years Charles would write letters in an attempt to smooth things over with his parents. Mom wrote back explaining that she missed him very much. Dad wasn't quite so understanding - his devout Christian principals were unwavering in his insistence that his son was now an adulterer, something he was completely unable to accept or condone.

Hillegas Hardware on Water Street, early 1900s

Jessie had written to her parent's hoping that they could find peace in the fact that she is finally, for the first time on her life, happy. There was no reply. Then there was the ex-husband and his propensity to violence and anger. There was always that feeling - and both of them felt it - that at any time Jessie's ex-husband would show up at their door waving a gun; for this reason they kept a very low profile. If that man loved Jessie even a fraction of what Charles did, there was nothing in the world that could stop him from finding her.

There is no hint that Charles had ever had major problems with his parents prior to their eruption over his plans with Jessie. It is for this reason that I believe Charles tried to smooth things over with them. If not for any other reason, there is the inheritance money...

Of course, Charles' mother would have been "the mother" – that is, she'd have found some common ground between herself and "her boy." Dad is another story. In Victorian America, Dad's were ridged, serious, and dominant. And, as we know from William's obituary, William was a devout Christian man. His obituary claims that William's life motto was "Better to suffer wrong, than do wrong." This does not sound like a man who would "look the other way" to heal the conflict with his son.

A Message Arrives

It was Monday, April 30th, 1906. There was knock on the door. It was the delivery of a telegram.

SENT: NAPERVILLE, ILLINOIS   USA

RECEIVER: HILLEGAS, CHARLES   HELENA, MONTANA

MSG:
PLEASE COME HOME -(STOP)-
FATHER DIED LAST NIGHT -(STOP)-

MOTHER INCONSOLABLE -(STOP)-
ASKING FOR YOU -(STOP)-

HARVEY HILLEGAS   6:45AM

***

> **W. H. Hillegas Summoned.**
>
> Citizens were surprised last Sunday night to hear that death had claimed our townsman, W. H. Hillegas. Heart failure was the immediate cause of death. Funeral services will be held from Zion church Thursday morning, May 3d; at 10 o'clock.

Newspaper announcement 1906

Charles was living in Montana at the time of his father's death in Naperville. A telegram would have been a common way to get a message out and received quickly. Of course, it is possible that he received a phone call instead.

Charles didn't say anything. In stunned shock, his hand went limp and the paper dropped to the ground. He vacantly backed away from the door. Jessie picked up the paper and read it. Without commenting she set it on a table. Then she put her arms around Charles. After a moment, she whispered, "He was a good man."

Charles stared off in the distance while nodding in agreement. "I should see Mom."

"Yes."

That day Charles was on the train bound for Naperville.

On Wednesday, May 2nd, Charles arrived in Naperville. He walked the few blocks from the depot on 4th Avenue to his mother's house on Front Street. Many members of the family were already there, comforting Mary. Charles was met with a cool reception as he walked into the house. His brother Harvey was there with his wife Jenette, along with Charles' sister Ida and her husband Simon. Other neighbors and members of Naperville's government and business community were also present. They all knew Charles, and the conditions under which he left his family. He didn't mind their opinions, besides they were right – he'd traded the love and acceptance of his family and hometown for the love of a divorced "sinner" named Jessie. And if he had it to do over again, he'd make the exact same decisions. Jessie was alive and vibrant; these people were small-minded and petty. He'd do anything to have Jessie with him; giving up Naperville and his family was a small price to pay. He hugged his mother and went up to his room to be alone.

William's funeral was held the next day, Thursday, May 3rd, 1906, partly under the supervision of the G.A.R. -The acronym stood for the Grand Army of the Republic, of which William was a member. (The G.A.R. was a fraternal organization of honorably discharged Union Civil War veterans).

Some of the rituals of the G.A.R. were based on the organization Freemasonry. The G.A.R. was founded in Decatur Illinois in 1866, and by 1890 they had over 400,000 men in membership. They were involved in charity and politics, and they lobbied for soldiers homes and pensions. The G.A.R. is responsible for the initiation of Decoration Day on May 30th, commonly referred to as Memorial Day.

The funeral was a large affair. William was waked in the front parlor of the house he'd built 36 years earlier. 40 comrades of the G.A.R. served as pallbearers and escort. The floral tributes were appropriate, varied, and beautiful. Because of William's influence and respect in the community, representatives from every church and level of society were in attendance for the service in the Zion church, as well, no business was allowed to be transacted, in Naperville, during William's funeral service.

Later at the graveside, the Grand Army burial service closed the obsequies of one who would long be remembered fondly and lovingly.

The details of the funeral service that are relayed here are from William's obituary that was printed in the Naperville Clarion newspaper, in 1906. William's complete newspaper obituary is reprinted in the Appendix herein.

The Talk that Changed Everything

As the funeral attendees dispersed from the graveside, Harvey approached Charles, "Have you got a minute to talk?"
Charles squinted at the morning sun shining through the trees. He continued walking and sighed a reluctant "Sure."
Harvey sensed the halfhearted attention and stepped in front of Charles to stop him. He looked him in the eye, "How long are you planning to stay in town?"
Charles looked around at the people leaving, he furled his brow, "Well, I'm not very welcome around here, but I'll stay as long as mom wants me to."
Harvey asked, "A few days?"
Charles snapped, "I don't know. Why do you care?"
Harvey looked over at his wife standing near William's open grave. She made eye contact with him and seemed to be losing patience waiting for him. Harvey took Charles by the arm and led him under a tree, away from his wife's view. He said, "I've been working for the last few month's with the artificial incubation of chickens, it's a fascinating science."
Charles smiled mockingly, "Seems somewhat beneath a Hillegas, -to keep company with filthy foul like a common... I don't know... farmer?"
"I agree. Dad wanted it. He thought there was money to be made with it."
"Maybe he was right."
"Maybe he was." He glanced at his father's newly dug grave, "Doesn't much matter anymore, does it?"
Charles shrugged his shoulders indifferently.
Harvey continued, "Besides, I think that whatever money dad was after, it is small potatoes compared to a discovery I inadvertently stumbled on with those filthy birds."
"Teach them to talk, did you?"
"No. Listen –"
Charles interrupted, "Good, they'd probably be foul-mouthed anyway."
Harvey rolled his eyes in disgust at the lame attempt at humor, "Do you remember those ridicules potions you and I used to experiment with?"
Charles got defensive, "They weren't ridicules. We had some worthwhile elixirs in there."

Harvey held up his hand as it to say 'enough'. "Sorry brother but they were ridicules. That is to say, all but one."

Charles was curious. "What are you getting at?"

"Sometimes, lately, when I was bored, I would go through our old notes, duplicate the potions, and feed them to the chickens, just to see how they would react. Most of the time nothing would happen. But, we had one mixture that was mostly banana, do you remember it?"

"Vaguely, yes."

"In our notes you wrote that it *was a pick-me-up potion. It was supposed to give massive amounts of energy to the weary.* So, I mixed a batch and ate some of it myself. I felt a bit dizzy from it. Then, using some of the leftover, I added a few more ingredients and gave some of if to one of the chickens."

Charles snapped, "And?"

"It died."

"It died?"

"Yeah. It was completely dead. I held it up, shook it, dunked it in water, nothing revived it. I had killed it with the new banana mixture!"

Charles was less than impressed. He snapped, sarcastically, "So, if everybody in America suddenly needs a quick way to kill all their chickens, they can buy our new banana potion to do it and we'll get rich?"

"No. Listen, I threw the dead chicken into a box thinking that I'd come back to him later and give it to mom to prepare him for a dinner. But, when I came back to get him a few hours later, he was alive!"

"So it was never really dead."

"No! It was dead. I'm positive!"

"How can a dead chicken come back to life? It doesn't make sense!"

"I thought the same thing. So, I killed a different chicken. Then, I crammed some of the banana potion down its throat."

"And?" Charles asked, losing patience.

"I waited."

"For what?"

"I didn't know..." Harvey took a deep breath, "A couple minutes later, it started moving."

Charles threw up his hands, "I've had enough. This is absurd." He started walking briskly toward Main Street. After a few seconds he turned back toward Harvey, shouting, "I'll be at the Pre-Emption House saloon, I need a drink!"

Pre-Emption HOUSE.

Corner Main and Water Streets.

Naperville, Illinois.

This hotel, established in 1835, and which has acquired such an honorable reputation in the past four years, during which time, we, its present Proprietors, have been connected with its management, has been lately re-fitted and remodelled, and is now one of the most popular on the C. B. & Q. R. R.

Our Hotel accommodations are ample, consisting of over thirty well furnished Bed-Rooms, two Sample Rooms, etc.

The "Pre-Emption House Stables" (as favorably known as the Hotel itself), are noted as the best within a circuit of ten miles around Naperville, containing stalls for over fifty horses, and affording shelter for a number of vehicles. An experienced hostler devotes his constant attention to the stables.

Board for men and horses, by the day or week, at reasonable rates. Meals furnished at any hour of the day, as desired.

STUTENROTH BROS.,

Daily Staging from this House for Warrenville and Winfield.

Naperville, August 2d, 1869.

Pre-Emption House ad

The folklore of Naperville tells us that Charles enjoyed mixing various potions, but there is no mention of Charles ever "messin around" with chickens. However, in April of 1906, just a few days before William died, there was a snippet in the Naperville newspaper, it says that *Harvey* Hillegas is learning the science of chicken incubation! So, Harvey was spending time with chickens on the Hillegas farm, not Charles. It certainly appears that both Charles and Harvey may have played around with potion mixing, but it was Harvey who discovered the "chicken resurrection" formula.

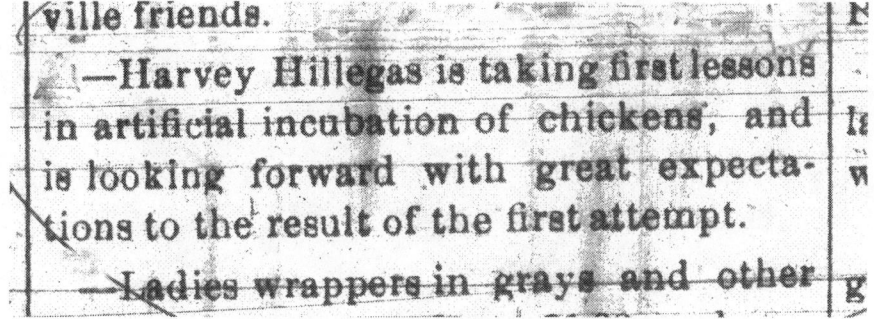

Newspaper snippet April 25, 1906

This also explains why Charles needed to come back to Naperville to get the formula -- because he didn't have the recipe for the "new" banana potion that Harvey had concocted.

If Charles had made the banana mixture previously, and believed that it brought dead things back to life, because why wouldn't he have used it on Jessie in Montana? The answer is that Charles didn't discover the life-giving potion, Harvey did.

So, when did Harvey tell Charles about the life-giving formula he'd discovered? Conversation between them would have been difficult, being that Charles and Harvey lived so far apart. I think the most logical opportunity would have been when they spent time together during their father's funeral.

If Harvey had a resurrection formula, why didn't they try it on his dead father? As far as Harvey was concerned that was a formula that brought chickens back from the dead, it hadn't been tried on a human and he no doubt respected his father too much to make him a guinea pig. It was only in Charles' desperation to get Jessie back, six years later, that the idea of an actual human resurrection was seriously considered.

When composing the dialog between Charles and Harvey in the cemetery, I took the approach that Charles is probably irritated being back in Naperville; he thought he had left it in his past for good. He probably couldn't wait to head back home to Jessie.

Also, I believe Charles looked down on his younger brother. Charles knew his brother wanted to move out west, but didn't, because of Dad's influence over him. Charles' opinion of Harvey is probably true, seeing that Harvey took off for the west coast before Dad's corpse had time to grow cold.

Charles has Unbelievable News

The Pre-Emption House was a Naperville saloon, hotel, restaurant, and stable all rolled into one. Located on the southeast corner of Main and Jackson, The Pre-Emption House was a popular stop for locals and travelers alike.

Charles entered the saloon and sat himself down at the bar. The bartender recognized him and announced to the entire place, "Hey! If it isn't old Charley Hillegas, come to pay us a visit!" Charles shook his head is disbelief, "Can I just get a whiskey, please? It's only 11am and it's already a rotten day."
The bartender poured a tall one, "I know, Chuck. Your daddy was a great man he'll be missed. This one is on me."
Charles raised the glass in toast to the bartender's generosity. As he drank it down, a handful of locals approached Charles, patted him on the back, and expressed their sorrow for his loss. Charles went through the motions.
"So Chuck, how's life in the wide open west?"
"It's quite a bit different than Naperville that's for sure."
"So, will you and Harvey be taking over the business of Hillegas Hardware?"
Charles laughed, "I'll be heading back home in a few days. I don't know about Harvey, we haven't discussed the store. He'll probably open a funeral parlor, if I know him!"
"The Beidelman brothers funeral parlor might have a problem with that! They hate competition!"
"Oh, my brother wouldn't be competing with them. He doesn't bury the dead; he brings them back to life! He says he's got a magic potion that brings things back from the dead!"
The entire saloon was now laughing and making fun of Harvey and the Hillegas Banana Potion. "Hey Charles, what makes you Hillegas boys think anyone would want to bring back their dead? Especially my mother in law!!"
The whole of the saloon was having a great time at the expense of Charles, Harvey, and a crazy story about a life-restoring banana potion. In the days that followed the whole town was laughing about the banana potion at the Hillegas place.

I believe that it was Charles talking about the life-giving potion that introduced the whole town to the banana portion and its claim to restore life.

The Beidelman brothers were one of the first undertaking establishments in Naperville, starting back in 1871. One can see where they might take issue with someone in town who can bring their clients back to life!

Beidelman Ad from early 1900s

Home Sweet Home

Charles was never so happy to see Jessie as he was when she met him at the Helena train station. It felt so good to put his arms around Jessie, and put Naperville - and its foolishness - behind him for good. In the days that followed he shared the story of Harvey's banana potion with Jessie and, they too, had a good laugh at Harvey's expense.

With Dad gone, Mom wrote Charles more frequently, keeping him up to date on developments in Naperville. Namely, she had decided to take over William's role in the affairs of Hillegas Hardware; after all, she needed something to keep her mind off the misery of her loss. Harvey, now that dad was gone, has decided that he and his wife Jenette will move out west - he's got his eye on Los Angeles. Ida, Simon, and the grandchildren will keep Mom company for the holidays and such.

Knowing that Mom was content in Naperville was a big load off of Charles' conscious. It was a good town, good people too, they would look after her. Charles knew that he and Jessie couldn't go back to Naperville permanently, even for Mom - just too much baggage there.

It would only be natural for Charles' mother to try to reestablish more communication with her estranged son now that she would be alone in Naperville, and since she didn't have to answer to William for doing so.

It is strange that neither of Mary's sons remained in Naperville to help her operate a large business concern like Hillegas Hardware. Especially Harvey, he had spent many years working the store with dear old Dad, and he knew the ropes - even Harvey's wife Jenette got in the act through the years, helping out in the store. But, now that Dad was gone, so was Harvey, leaving mom to fend for herself.

> —Mrs. Harvey Hillegas is presiding over the Naperville Merchants Rebate Check Association's stock of wares given in exchange for red stamps issued by said association and given to cash paying patrons. Headquarters has been established in Hillegas' hardware store. The articles embraced in the display are both useful and ornamental and make quite an attractive exhibition of merchandise.

Snippet from the newspaper showing that Jenette helped out in Hillegas Hardware, Nov. 1899

Mary did have family in nearby towns: we know that Ida wasn't too far from her mom. Ida died in Maywood Illinois in 1948 (the distance between Naperville and Maywood was only 24 miles). The Hillegas family also had relatives in Elgin Illinois (about 25 miles from Naperville), we know there were relatives in Elgin because a newspaper snippet mentions that Ida "is spending time with relatives in Elgin."

The End of the Road

It had been five years since dad passed, and life for Charles and Jessie continued as a blessing. As they approached their 10-year anniversary, November 1st, 1911, they reveled in, each other, the happiness that they've shared, and the future of their love. They loved each other more today than they did on their wedding day - 10 years ago in that old Butte, Montana courthouse; the bond of their affections actually grew stronger with time. They knew now that nothing could ever separate them, *ever*.

We know the lengths to which Charles would soon go to keep Jessie in his life; they were still, quite obviously, very much in love when she died.

A Promise Made

In April of 1912 Jessie began to grow ill. Day by day she was weaker and sicker. She felt so very sick. Then, on May 1st, 1912, Jessie Hillegas closed her eyes for the last time. Charles held tightly to her hands - they gradually grew cold in his grasp. At the tender age of just 36, ten years into her marriage to Charles, Jessie Robateene Massey-Hillegas slipped into eternity on a Spring day in the beautiful state of Montana.

The exact date of Jessie's death is unknown, even though cemetery records claim it is May 6th, 1912. We know the 6th is incorrect because her remains arrived in Naperville on May 6th, so she probably died four to six days earlier. There isn't a Death Certificate for Jessie in either Montana or Washington. We checked – as did the Naperville Historical Society – and could find nothing to substantiate Jessie's actual death date or official cause of death. Even the Naperville Cemetery, where Jessie is buried, has no records of the details of her death.

Being a trained medical professional, Chuck Kennedy has determined that Jessie probably died of either Consumption or Influenza; both were very common causes of death to the young at the turn of the century. Jessie probably didn't die from the Spanish Flu that killed millions in the early part of the 20th century, because it didn't erupt until 1918, six years after Jessie's death.

The depth of Charles' sorrow was too deep for him to bear; his only reason to live was gone. He stared at her lifeless shell, praying that she'd awake - praying it was just a nightmare. He begged her to come back to him. "Please God, I will do anything to have her back. Please?" Jessie remained lifeless and still. Charles rambled to himself, "There must be a way to bring her back. There must be - " -Charles stopped in mid-sentence. His memory went back to his father's graveside, in the Naperville Cemetery, six years ago, to the conversation he had with his brother Harvey...

"The potion brought back life..."

"I know the chicken was dead, I'm positive. But, somehow, it was alive again..."

"All our elixirs were garbage, except one... I tweaked it, and it brings back the dead."

"Do you remember your banana potion..."

"I now it sounds crazy, but it worked - it brings back the dead..."

As Charles gazed at the remains of his dear wife his desperation grew. Somewhere in that desperation he remembered the life-giving formula.

Charles' mind was reeling: '*What if Harvey was right? What if the formula that he concocted does bring the dead back to life?*' Charles began pacing the floor frantically, asking himself out loud, "How can I bury Jessie without knowing for sure if the potion would bring her back? I can't bury her until I know. I have to know. I must try the potion on Jessie. Jessie, I promise you, I will try..."

Charles turned and looked in the dresser mirror, his eyes were red and bloodshot from crying, his mouth uncontrollably quivering from heartbreak and hopelessness. He stared into the reflection of his own eyes. He reached his hand up to the mirror, and, touching his hand's reflection, he stared intently into his own eyes as he spoke to himself in the mirror. "I will bring her back... I will bring her back... I can do this... " Then he turned to Jessie, lying lifeless on the bed, he said, "In my mother's house are my notes. In the notes may be your life. Harvey was probably wrong, but we have to try. I have to find those notes to discover how Harvey tweaked my formula."

Charles walked out into the hallway of the boardinghouse. There he lifted the telephone earpiece from its resting place. He put the receiver to his ear and spoke into the mouthpiece, "Ahoy, operator? Can you connect me to the town of Naperville? It's in Illinois. Yes, number 361. Please hurry."

Telephone, 1912

After a moment someone picked up the line, Charles responded, "Hello, Mother? Charles. Not so good mom. I've lost Jessie. Just a few minutes ago. No, she's been very sick for a while. I'd like to bring her to Naperville, to our family plot, with your permission. Thank you. We'll leave right away." Charles hung up the phone. He went back to their room and sat down on the bed next to Jessie. He lovingly brushed her hair from her face. Then he leaned over and whispered in her ear, "Jess, *we're going home.*"

This scene is meant to illustrate what I believe happened to Charles – because of his desperation, he lost touch with reality. He began to feel that as impossible as it was that the formula would bring Jessie back to life, he had no choice but to try. He reasoned, *How could he bury her without trying the formula* ? He realized that if he simply dismissed the formula as ludicrous and buried her in Montana without trying it, he would question himself about the decision every minute for the rest of his life. *He had no choice but to try.* Perhaps it was being put into this bizarre situation that ultimately pushed him over the edge?

We have to assume Charles secured his mother's permission prior to bringing Jessie back home to Naperville to be buried in the family plot. At that time the Hillegas home phone number was 361, according to a phonebook from the time. We can also assume he lost no time calling mom - if he was to try to bring Jessie back to life, every second that passed reduced his chance for success.

Naperville phone book showing Hillegas home number in 1912

Sunday, May 5th, 1912

The three-day journey from Montana seemed like a million years. Charles kept telling himself that soon they would be back in Montana, he and Jessie happy again, together. All he has to do is get her to Naperville, find the notes, mix Harvey's banana concoction, feed it to Jessie, and then...

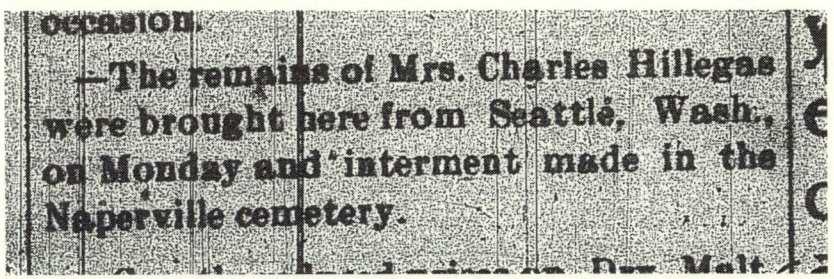

Snippet from the newspaper May 6, 1912

The sun was setting behind him as Charles noticed the Naperville depot growing larger out his window; the journey from Montana to Naperville was almost over.

As he disembarked the train, representatives of Beidelman's Undertaking establishment of Naperville met Charles. They carefully removed the casket from the train and loaded it into their motor hearse for the short transport to the location of tomorrow's funeral service, the home of Charles' mother.

Mary met her heartbroken son Charles at the front door, as he entered, a cool spring breeze blew through the house. The casket was brought in right behind him and set up in the front parlor of house for the service. Seeing the casket in the front parlor of the house conjured memories of William's funeral service in the home just six years ago. Jessie's funeral service would begin tomorrow morning, 9am. Charles didn't have much time. He had to find his notes, mix the elixir, and feed it to Jessie, all before 9am tomorrow. He had a quick dinner with his mother and retired to his room.

The first thing to do was to find the notes. Charles tore his room apart looking for the notebook, no success. Harvey had it last - maybe it was in his room somewhere? Charles snuck into Harvey's old room, being extra quiet so as not to wake up mom. He began to rummage through Harvey's belongings - no success. Was it on Harvey's bookshelf? No. *Damn him, where could he have put it?* Charles searched the house late into the night without finding the notebook. *Maybe Harvey destroyed it? Maybe he'd brought it with him to California? Damn...*

It was early twilight when Charles gave up his search and went into the parlor. Jessie's casket lay in the dark, on a beautifully decorated table in the corner. He walked up to it and put his hand on it, sighing, "I have failed you. I'm sorry." He sat down on the sofa, pulled a small blanket over himself, and closed his weary eyes.

The next thing he knew his mother was next to him, jostling him from his slumber. She tapped him on the knee and whispered, "God bless you Charles, I pray that the good Lord gives you strength. There are few things on this earth as difficult as laying a loved one to rest. You're a good son." He put his arms around her to warm her up; the room was cool. After a moment, she stood up, already exasperated, and sighed, "Come now, we've a long day ahead of us..."

At this point he probably felt like he'd let her down; but at least he tried – he got her to Naperville, he tore the house apart looking for the formula, it wasn't there - what else could he do?

No doubt the only thing on Charles' mind, upon arriving in Naperville, was finding the recipe for the banana concoction. He knew his own recipe, but Harvey claimed to have tweaked it. It was that "tweak" that had thrown Charles a curve ball. He had to find out what Harvey had done to the original formula that gave it the life-giving quality.

Charles couldn't ask Harvey because Harvey wasn't in Naperville in 1912, he was living in Los Angeles California with his wife Jenette. Also, I think their brother/brother relationship was angry, at best.

The reason this account has Charles failing Jessie is that *something* prevented Charles from giving the formula to Jessie prior to her burial. It most certainly would have been easier to give it to her four days after she died and before she was buried, than it was to give it to her almost two weeks after death and having to dig her up to do it! So, the question is: what stopped him? Our conclusion is that he couldn't find the recipe and had to go ahead with her burial. Curiously though, he didn't stop looking for the notebook! Even after burying her he kept looking for it and eventually found it. Of course, after finding the notebook, Charles was faced with a huge problem: Jessie is now two weeks dead and six feet in the ground! He's still determined to bring her back.

In this account, I've made Charles' mother forgiving and supportive of him in a Christian capacity because her obituary clearly states over and over that she was guided in her life by a fervent Biblical Christian belief system.

It wasn't unusual for Naperville funerals at the turn of the century to be held in the parlor of a home, even though Beidelman's Funeral Home in Naperville did have a funeral chapel on Washington Street. It is our contention that Charles would have opted for his mother's house for the wake/funeral so that he had access to Jessie's remains at all times. Note: Charles' funeral 28 years later would be held in the Beidelman's chapel on Washington Street.

Beidelman funeral parlor on Washington, now retail

I chose to conclude that Jessie's vault was of a "simple construction." This because in a few days Charles is going to break it open to remove Jessie from it. Because he is successful in breaking it open, I am of the opinion that it couldn't have been one of the virtually indestructible and "fortified" units that were available at the time.

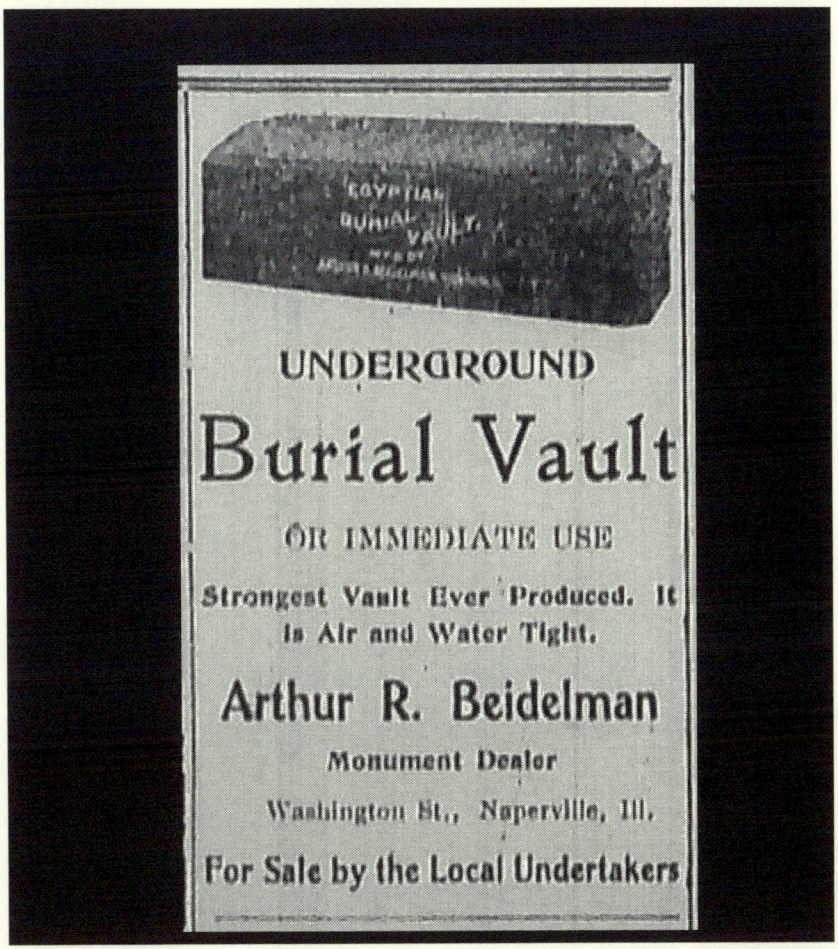

One of the virtually indestructible types of vaults available in Naperville in 1912

Monday, May 6, 1912

As Charles had expected, the funeral gathering was slight; he and Jessie weren't looked upon with much respect in Naperville. Still, Jessie received a better send off than she'd have gotten had Charles buried her in Montana. The Hillegas family burial plot was large, and located in a beautiful section of the Naperville Cemetery on Washington Street.

Charles wasn't sure that dad would have agreed to Jessie's inclusion in the family plot, but mom did, and hers was the only voice that mattered on this cool May morning. The minister said a few kind words in the parlor of the house as well as in the blustery morning breezes graveside. Jessie was laid to rest ten feet north of her father-in-law William in the Naperville Cemetery.

I'd bet that during Jessie's funeral service Charles looked over at his Dad's tombstone and had to try not to laugh at dear old Dad. William wanted nothing to do with Jessie, because she was divorced. But here was Charles, not only laying Jessie in the Hillegas family plot that William bought "for family," but he was laying Jessie to rest just ten short feet from dad – for all time. *And there was nothing that Dad could do about it.*

Jessie never legally divorced her first husband, which meant that Charles was married to another man's wife. *And no doubt both of them took that secret to their graves.* **No one was to ever know about the bigamy – until *now*.**

Following the service, Charles, his sister Ida, her husband Simon, and Mom, went back to the Hillegas house on Front Street. Charles went right up to his room to think about his future. *What to do now? Should he stay here in Naperville and help Mom with the store? Should he head back to Seattle, where he lived before marrying Jessie? How could he possibly carry on at all without her?* - So many things to sort out.

As Charles lay there on his bed, he began to think about his youth; so many lazy afternoons were spent laying on this bed thinking about mixing herbs and roots into new elixirs. Dad thought he and Harvey were crazy – maybe they were. They used to spend so much time in the barn mixing potions...
The barn?
Charles jumped to his feet. *The barn!*
He hadn't looked for the notebook in the barn!
He rushed down the stairs and out the back door, tripping over himself to get to the barn as fast as he could. When he got there, he threw a door open... - The afternoon light crept in, filling the darkness. Off to the side was a workbench, piled high with years of junk and dirt. Charles began to quickly clear away the debris.

It only took a few seconds. There it was: the notebook.

Charles grabbed it and ran out into the yard, for the sunlight. He frantically turned the pages looking for the mixture Harvey had talked about – something to do with banana...

He neared the end of the notebook without finding it, *damn, had Harvey removed it? Wait, there's one that looks interesting...* Charles tried to make out his faded writing. *This one claims that it cures weariness and increases energy – and the primary ingredient is banana. This is it! This is the one! This is the elixir Harvey was talking about! There are additional ingredients in the recipe that are written in Harvey's hand. There is writing on the page bottom from Harvey as well...*

It reads:

Using Chuck's energy elixir as a base, I adjusted the formula in the recipe as noted above. In my experiments with chicken incubation, I fed this new mixture to several of the chickens. I am stunned to submit here that something very peculiar happened.

It sounds unthinkable, even blasphemous, but this new mixture of mine appears to reanimate life in the lifeless.

Harvey Hillegas, 1906

Charles closed the notebook. He sat down in the grass. Time seemed to stand still as he contemplated his options. '*This is the mixture that could bring Jessie back to me. This is the mixture that can change everything. I've got it. But in order to try it, I'll have to remove Jess from her grave and bring her back here, to the barn...*'

We know that Charles didn't find the formula until after Jessie was buried; this is evidence by the fact the he didn't try the mixture on her until after she'd been buried. As I contemplated this situation, I reasoned that the barn is most likely the place Charles didn't think of to look for the notebook initially, while most certainly he'd have thought to tear the whole house apart in his search. It also makes sense that if Harvey was experimenting with chicken incubation; the experiments were probably going on in the barn. So the notebook could have easily had a place on a shelf in the barn, or just piled in dirty barn junk.

The Impossible Plan

Charles went up to his room clutching the notebook under his arm. He laid on his bed thinking, '*If I'm going to do this, it has to be as soon as possible.*' He took a deep breath, leapt from his bed, and headed down to the kitchen to secure the ingredients for the elixir. Then, he returned to his bedroom and followed the "recipe" meticulously.

It only took a few moments to produce. He held it up to the light, as he whirled the mixture in the cup; it was yellow and thick, and smelled like bananas – certainly didn't look like it could work miracles. He then hid the cup of elixir from his mother's view by tucking it under his shirt as he made his way out to the barn.

He set the cup on a shelf and began looking around the barn for the equipment he'd need to get Jessie back to the barn. He secured a shovel, a lantern, and a two-wheeled cart. Confident in his success, he made a comfortable place in the hay for Jessie to lie down. Then, he went up to his bed to wait for an opportunity to slip away unnoticed.

We are told in the Naperville Clarion newspaper, from May of 1912, in a story about the grave robbing, that Charles attempted to rob the grave on Saturday, May 11th, 1912. So he must have had the formula ready to go before that. There is no way for us to know if any of his delay was Charles simply trying to build up his nerve.

As Charles thought about the project that lay ahead, he had to secure provisions and provide for Jessie's comfort. We are told that Jessie was found in a partially standing position (this information was in the Wheaton Illinoisian newspaper following the grave robbing). Charles must have prepared a place for her in order for the remains to be propped in such a fashion.

Charles no doubt felt that a shovel would be necessary for digging - we know he had this with him. The bringing of a lantern and a cart for this first foray to the cemetery are speculation at this point. But, we do know he had these items with him on his second excursion,

it's probably reasonable to assume that he had them the first time also.

<u>Saturday, May 11, 1912</u>

Five days had passed since Jessie's burial. Charles was going crazy with the stress of implementing his plan; he'd been waiting for a perfect time to slip away, but he couldn't put it off any longer. He resolved that tonight he would see it the plan through.

As the sun set and Naperville grew dark, Charles knew that his Mother would soon be retiring for the night. Soon, he heard her footsteps coming up the stairs; then they sounded as if they were coming toward his room. Soon a gentle wrap echoed on his door.

He said, "Yes?"

His Mother pushed the door open and peered in, "Goodnight Charles. It's difficult to believe, I know, but tomorrow will be a better day."

Charles nodded, "Thanks. Goodnight."

She turned and slowly made her way to her room and closed the door. Charles jumped up and quietly rushed outside to the barn.

The night was cold. Charles looked around to make sure none of the neighbors were outside - *he was alone.* He grabbed the shovel, lantern, and cart. As he headed out, he stopped to think which three-quarter-mile route to the cemetery would be best. *Ellsworth Avenue south to Chicago Avenue would be fine to get to the cemetery but the steepness of Fort Hill will be too difficult on the return trip, pushing the cart with Jessie in it. He could cut through Central Park to Washington Street, and take Washington down to the cemetery. That would be fine to get to the cemetery, but Washington Street is too busy to get Jessie back home without being noticed. The only way he could determine - the way that would provide him level streets and privacy - would be to cut through Central Park, go west on Van Buren Avenue to Main Street. Then take the quiet side street Main south to the cemetery. The reverse route would work too.* He was happy with that plan.

He ducked down as low as he could and began his three-quarter-mile trek to the Naperville Cemetery.

We know that there were no witnesses to Charles heading out of the house, on the night of the first attempt. -- At least no one has ever come forward.

The ¾ mile route that Charles took from his barn to the cemetery is an interesting study. Most of the streets available to him in 1912 would have been somewhat busy and he could have easily been stopped by law enforcement – especially on his way back with a corpse. Chuck Kennedy and I worked out every possible route he could have taken, and it is our opinion that he headed west, cutting through the Park that is conveniently located right behind his barn. He took Van Buren Avenue west two blocks to Main Street. This is a good choice for him because it cuts through the business district, which is of course, closed at night, and very quiet. Naperville has a river that runs through it, between Charles' barn and the Naperville Cemetery. So he needs a road that will provide a bridge over the river, Main Street has a bridge. He can turn left (south) onto Main off of Van Buren and make a straightaway to the cemetery and Jessie's grave. Part of it is uphill as he nears Hillside Road, but that's just when he's going to the cemetery, obviously, it will be an easy downhill on the way back with Jessie.

To those familiar with Naperville Streets, another route may occur to you: Perhaps Charles used an eastern street such as Sleight to get south to Hillside, from there he may have headed west to Washington Street and there entered the cemetery. While this sounds plausible today, it wouldn't have been an option for Charles in 1912, because Hillside Road didn't extend from the east side of Naperville through to Washington Street. The extension of Hillside Road to Washington occurred in about 1953 to give easy access to Washington Street to the residents of a new subdivision called: The Highlands. The bridge on Hillside - that crosses over river - was built at the same time as the road.

The cemetery was pitch dark. Charles lit his lantern to help him find his way to Jessie's grave. The ground at her grave was cold, but soft, loose, and freshly turned, as he sank the shovel into the dirt. With each shovel-full he made his way closer to her. He could almost hear her calling to him. His heartbeat was driving him to a frenzy. His breathing grew rapid and shallow. He kept telling himself, "*Keep going, keep going.*"

Just then an angry voice came from the darkness, "Hey! What business have you here?"

Charles' heart skipped a beat. He looked up, paniced, from his macabre task.

There, a man - the cemetery sexton - stood in front of him. "Well, damned fool, what's your business?"

Charles was speechless, defenseless.

The man held up his lantern to illuminate the trespasser's face. He could see by the fear in Charles' eyes that he had been driven mad, insane even. Fearing for his own safety, the sexton quickly defused the confrontational aspect of the situation and said, "You'll need a permit to remove a body from its grave, maybe you should get one."

Charles jumped at the opportunity, "I'll return with that then."

They parted company without further trouble. Charles went home thinking that the situation was over; the sexton however wasn't about to let a possible grave robbing go unreported.

The Wheaton Illinoisian newspaper story on the grave robbing tells us that Charles was caught trying to rob the grave on his first attempt, Saturday, May 11th. It tells us that the sexton confronted Charles. But, fearing that he was "not right" (and probably a bit dangerous,) told Charles that a permit would be necessary to remove a body from its grave. Charles told him that he'd return with the permit.

The sexton then quickly made his way to the home of Oliver Beidelman, a prominent Naperville undertaker. He informed Oliver Beidelman of the peculiar events that had transpired in the cemetery. Mr. Beidelman, being a Hillegas family friend, and wanting to spare them any more trouble, told the sexton, "Don't tell the sheriff about this, I'll take care of it myself." The sexton obliged.

The next day, Sunday, May 12, 1912, Beidelman paid a visit to Mrs. Hillegas, informing her of Charles' actions in the cemetery the previous evening. He told her that Charles is undoubtedly going mad with the stress of his loss. He is losing reason and must be watched closely. Mrs. Hillegas agreed.

This part of the story, in which a Beidelman intercedes on behalf of the Hillegas family, is part of the folklore of the story – we, at this point, can't prove or disprove it. I include it in the story for two reasons:

1) Because it makes sense that the sexton would want to report this bizarre situation to *someone*. The sexton probably worked very closely with Beidelman and sought his advice in the matter.

2) In the Naperville Clarion newspaper story about the grave robbing, it states that Charles was caught trying to rob the grave; it goes on to say '*since then he has been carefully watched.*' The newspaper however doesn't tell us how he came to be watched. In other words, who "told" on him? Somehow the fact that he was in the cemetery, and caught robbing the grave, had to be reported to someone, by someone. We are left to speculate how this occurred. However, the piece of folklore concerning the intercession of Beidelman is a puzzle piece solution that fits this quandary. Concerning this theory we've no proof at this point.

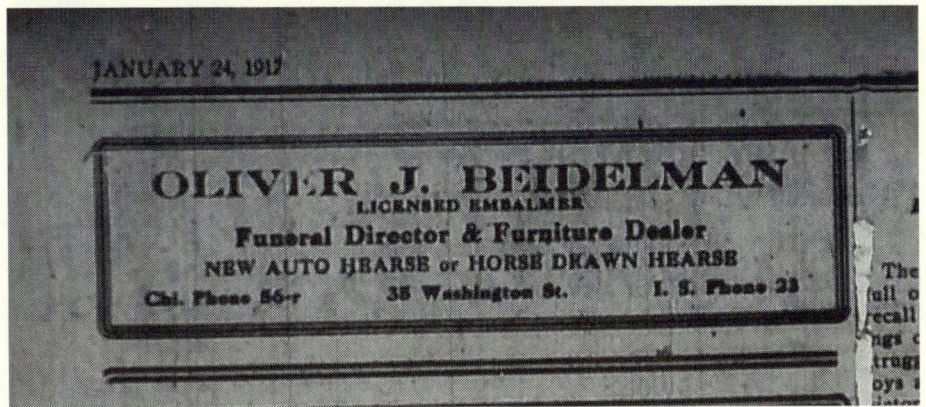

Beidelman Funeral Home ad - 1912

When Charles' mother asked him later that day why he had done such a horrid thing, Charles - unable to tell her that his plan was to bring Jessie back from the dead - said, "I had a vision that she was still alive." Mrs. Hillegas assured him that Jessie, having been in her casket for over a week now, is most surely with the departed. Charles nodded in reluctant agreement. Mrs. Hillegas felt confident that Charles now understood the reality of his wife's passing. But, what she didn't realize is that he had every intention of succeeding in his secret objective – to bring his wife Jessie back from the dead.

He just needs another chance...

We are told in the Naperville Clarion newspaper story that Charles had had a vision that his wife was still alive, and that this vision promptly panicked him and caused his excursion into the cemetery with the shovel. This information about the vision had to have come to the newspaper from his mother, because, who could he have told this lie to other than his mother?

Of course, there is the possibility that Charles didn't say he had a vision at all! Perhaps his mother was lying to the newspaper in an attempt to in someway justify his actions to the public.

Monday, May 13, 1912

Charles knew he had to devise a new plan, and quick. The only way he was going to get Jessie was to elude the sexton, but how? He was racking his brain for a solution so hard that exhaustion set in and all he wanted to do was sleep. And that's when it hit him - *the sexton has to eventually go to sleep tonight!* That was Charles' mistake last time - the sexton hadn't yet retired for the night. *'Tonight,'* Charles thought, *'tonight, I'll watch his light. When his room goes dark, Jessie will be mine.'*

Charles stayed in bed until he was sure all of Naperville was sound asleep. Then he slinked out to the barn and secured the equipment he'd had last time. This time though there was an added guarantee for success: a gun. This time, no one is going to stop him - No one. He slipped the gun in his belt and stealthy made his way to the cemetery. As he entered the cemetery grounds he hid behind a tree and glanced over to the sexton's quarters – the light was off. Surely he was asleep by now, it's past 11. As an added precaution, Charles won't light his lantern unless he absolutely needs to. He, then, quietly, stumbled, in the pitch dark, over to Jessie's grave.

The Wheaton Illinoisian newspaper account of the grave robbery tells us that Charles "dug up wife's body while sexton slept."

He waited a few minutes for his vision to adjust to the extreme darkness in the center of the cemetery where Jessie's grave was. He knelt in the fresh dirt and whispered, "Don't be afraid Jess, it's just me." He grabbed the shovel and sank it in the dirt.

With every shovel-full the grave opened larger and Charles was a little closer to Jessie. This time, unlike a few days ago, Charles was being much more deliberate and careful; making sure he stayed hidden and quiet.

As the grave grew deeper it also grew darker near its bottom and Charles concluded that he had no choice but to light his lantern. He realized that doing so was to broadcast his presence to any passers-by, but there was no way he could continue so deep in the ground without light. He stuck a match and lit the lantern.

He placed the light at ground level, grabbed the shovel, and jumped back down into the empty earth. The lantern was doing its job; he could see that he didn't have that much further to go. It was than that he heard something, out in the dark. His heart skipped a beat, as he grabbed his gun. Was he caught again? *No one is stopping me, no one.* His finger tightened around the trigger. He stood still. He could hear people talking. It sounded like it was coming from Hillside Road. Maybe kids? He held perfectly still. The voices gradually began to fade off in the distance. Within a moment, they were gone and hadn't noticed him. He heaved a heavy sigh of relief as he looked at the gun in his hand – *he was losing control, this was driving him insane.*

In a Naperville Sun newspaper story, in 1972, an 81-year-old Naperville resident named Pete Schrader tells the story of how he and a friend inadvertently stumbled on Charles in the midst of his second attempt. As Pete (who was at the time of the grave robbing 21-years-old), relates the event, it goes like this: He and a friend had been out catching bullfrogs at a local lake. At around midnight, they started walking home. As they walked down Hillside Road, which borders the cemetery, they noticed what looked like a light, or lantern, in the center of the cemetery. They didn't give it much thought until they heard the next day that Charles Hillegas had robbed his wife's grave the previous night. Pete then realized that the light they saw in the cemetery was Charles robbing his wife's grave.

This story helps us a couple ways: It tells us what time Charles was in the cemetery, and it tells us that he had a lantern lit.

With that close call Charles knew that he had to finish quickly, he took a deep breath and yet again thrust the shovel into the ground. But instead of the familiar sound of the blade piercing dank dirt, the hallow sound of wood echoed in Charles' ears. Realizing that he'd hit the top of the rough box that contained Jessie's casket, he stopped cold, threw the shovel down, and fell on his knees. He began to frantically sweep dirt away from the rough box lid. The damp dirt caked under his fingernails. He reached around to find the lid's edges and cleared the dirt away so he could get a grip on it. Then, bracing himself against the edges of the grave, he suspended his body over the box and gave the lid an adrenalin-induced yank. The wood cracked and creaked as the rough box lid surrendered its seal to Charles' determination. There, beneath him, lay Jessie's casket. He stepped onto the casket for stability, and maniacally ripped the rough box lid from its base. He tossed it up and out to ground level.

We are told in the Wheaton Illinoisian newspaper account of the event, that Jessie was in a casket, and the casket was in a "rough box," probably to protect it from the elements. We also know from that story that Charles used the lid of the rough box like a litter, or stretcher, to support Jessie on her journey from the cemetery to the barn.

It was a bit tricky working out how Charles was able to break into the rough box (without breaking the lid apart completely). And then, how did he proceed to remove Jessie from her casket? Bear in mind also that all this was accomplished in very limited light and work area. I believe the description I've written, of the grave robbing, would be very close to what actually happened considering there wasn't much room in the hole for many other variables.

Charles was balancing himself over the casket, standing on the edges of the rough box. He reached down with his right hand and slowly pulled Jessie's casket open... The pungent and foul aroma of human putrefaction poured into the open grave. Charles began to cough, gasp, and gag. His eyes were watering. It was so dark. He felt dizzy. He reached for the lantern...

As the soft glow of the flame illuminated the interior of the grave, Jessie came into full view for Charles. She lay so still – as if sleeping. Her hands folded together on her stomach, fingers intertwined as if in prayer. He brought the lantern close to her, near her shoulders. Her once-beautiful face was sunken, drawn, and white. Her once-full lips were thin, blue, and cracked. The only remnant of her former beauty was her long brown hair; even in this surreal moment her gorgeous brown main surrounded her peaceful face and fell gracefully down on her shoulders.

Charles didn't see the decay. Looking into the casket, he only saw his beautiful bride - as glorious to him as on their wedding day. A tear fell from Charles' face to Jessie's. How much he had been missing her...

At this point Jessie has been dead for about two weeks. The fact that Charles pressed on despite what Jessie must have looked like, and smelled like, suggests to me that he was oblivious to it all and only saw the gorgeous woman he loved.

He set the lantern up at ground level and took a deep breath of fresher air. He then stepped into the casket holding the lid open with his left leg. He bent over and unclasped Jessie's hands from each other. He wrapped her arms around his neck. He then slipped his hands under her shoulders and gently lifted her up from her casket. She seemed so cold and fragile. He lifted her higher as he slipped his left hand behind her, now cradling her in his arms. He paused for a moment and hugged her tightly, to warm her up, before raising her high and gently setting her out onto the ground level with a deep grunt.

Charles climbed out of the grave and sat on the ground beside Jessie – his heart was racing; he was nauseous, confused, and out of breath. He extinguished the lantern and - sitting in the dark - tried to gather his thoughts.

Exhausted, Charles reached for the two-wheeled cart he'd brought. He propped it upright next to Jessie. As he gently sat her in it, it was clear to him that it wasn't going to be practical – her arms and legs were hanging over the edges of the cart in a most "un-lady-like" way. Charles knew he didn't have the energy to carry her home either. He let out a frustrated sigh, "Damn." It was then that he noticed the rough box lid lying off to the side of the open grave. It gave him an idea.

He laid the lid over the top of the cart and then gently laid Jessie upon it, like a make shift stretcher. She looked much more "comfortable." He then moved the cart, with Jessie aboard, toward Hillside Road, to test it for stability. It seemed to be working. He grabbed his lantern and shovel and quickly began pushing the loaded cart across Hillside and north, down Main Street, en route back to his Mom's house, ¾ of a mile away.

We are told in the Wheaton Illinoisian newspaper story that Charles had used the lid of the rough box like a litter, or stretcher, on the cart.

As he made his way through Central Park, he could see, in a short distance ahead of him, his mother's barn. He felt great relief; he'd made it without getting caught.

Pulling the barn door open he went inside and lit the lantern. In the corner of the barn was the resting place he'd prepared for Jessie, it was a small pile of hay and looked satisfactory. He pulled the cart into the dimly lit barn stopping next to the small pile of hay. He then lifted Jessie from the rough box lid, and, while cradling her in his arms, he laid her down gently in the hay. Charles thought Jessie looked comfortable but he could see that the position of Jessie laying flat on her back wasn't going to work – in order to "feed" her, she'd need to be more propped up. Charles reached for the rough box lid. He stood it up behind Jessie with its top edge leaning against a barn support post. He then lifted Jessie into a partially standing position and leaned her against the lid. It worked.

We are told in the Wheaton Illinoisian newspaper story that Jessie was found in the barn in a partially standing position, leaning on the rough box lid.

Charles wiped the stress-induced sweat from his brow and reached for the cup that held the banana elixir...

Feeding Time

A faint ray of moonlight shone through the partially open barn door, the soft blue light fell softly across Jessie. Charles set the cup on the dirt floor as he knelt down next to her. He stared at her for a moment in disbelief – he couldn't believe she was here, in the barn – he had her all to himself. He looked down at the cup of potion, then back to Jessie's pale white face. Unsure how to proceed, he took a deep breath, gathered his nerve, and improvised the process: He cupped her face in his hands lovingly. Then, delicately he pushed his two thumbs into the corners of her mouth and pried her jaws apart. Her mouth fell open, almost invitingly.

Charles gulped, in surreal disbelief, this was it: the moment of truth. He whispered, "Whatever happens, I love you Jess, more than anything." He reached down and picked up the cup of potion, then he picked up a small nearby stick. He stirred the mixture in the cup with the stick for a moment and tossed the stick aside.

Holding the cup in his left hand, he reached over to the back of Jessie's head with his right hand. He grabbed her hair at the scalp and lovingly pulled it down to tip her head backward. Her mouth opened further, and her throat appeared wide. Charles put the cup edge to Jessie's lips and slowly poured the potion into Jessie's mouth. Her mouth filled quickly and the potion overflowed out onto Jessie's face. Charles stopped pouring to wait for the elixir the seep down her throat. After a moment her open mouth was drained of the potion and Charles again filled it with what remained in the cup. He waited a moment for her to "swallow" it all, and then, calmly, he pushed up on her lower jaw causing her mouth to close somewhat. He did it. It wasn't the neatest job – he'd spilled some of the potion on Jessie's face, neck, and dress. But that didn't concern him; the important thing is that Jessie drank most of it. He sighed, "It has to work. It has to… "

The cup is in Charles' left hand because his signature tells us that he was left handed.

Naperville folklore tells us that Jessie had "banana" on her mouth, face, and clothes.

Charles kissed Jessie's forehead and snuggled up next to her to warm her up. He took one of her hands into his and he waited, all the while watching Jessie's hand very closely; waiting for it to twitch, move, or grab hold of his hand. Several minutes went by and her hand only seemed to grow colder. He pressed the back of her hand to his cheek and said, "You can do this Jess. Come back to me. Come back Jess. Please come back. Please God. Bring her back."

As the hours passed, Charles felt the reality of failure sinking into his heart; with each moment he lost a little more hope.

Tuesday, May 14, 1912 – Early Morning

As the dawn of the new day was breaking, Charles was still holding out a small hope that Jessie would come back, that her eyelids would soon flutter, that she - in her soft voice, as if rising from a prolonged slumber - would very soon whisper his name. All his attention was focused intently on Jessie, watching for any sign of reanimation.

Just then Charles was startled as the barn door began to painfully creak as it slowly opened. Charles looked toward the door, realizing it to be his mother. She looked into the dark barn, straining to see in the limited light, "Charles are you in here?" She stepped in, "You weren't in your room, I thought maybe..." Her voice trailed off in shock as she saw Charles sitting in the hay. Beside him, Jessie - propped up, partially standing.

"Dear God..."

The Wheaton Illinoisian newspaper tells us that Charles' mother looked in the barn for him when she realized that he wasn't in his bedroom - She feared that he was in trouble. The paper also tells us that it was at this point that she saw Jessie in the barn, propped up in a partially standing position, leaning against the rough box lid.

Charles was caught off guard. He grabbed his gun and pointed it at his mom. He wanted her out. *He needs more time. He couldn't give up on Jessie, not now. He just needs a little more time. Just a little more time.* He screamed, "Get out!"

In shocked disbelief she shook her head, unable to comprehend what she was seeing, "Charles? Charles, what have you done?"

His eyes grew wild and defensive. He stood up and aggressively approached her, all the while pointing the gun at her. "I said, get out! Now! Get out!"

She turned and ran to the door in terror, "I'm getting the sheriff..."

"Get out!"

Charles could hear her crying as she ran back to the house.

He looked down at the gun in his hand. He felt ashamed that he'd pointed it at his mother. He looked over to Jessie - nothing had changed. He felt his heart break. He heaved a heavy sigh, "It's over."

The Wheaton Illinoisian paper tells us that she hastily notified authorities about Charles' actions. It doesn't tell us that he pointed a gun at her, but it does say that he was "brandishing a gun." Since none of the law enforcement dealt with Charles at the barn, to whom was he brandishing the gun? It must have been his mom, when she discovered him.

At this point Charles' failure was imminent, his time was up. He knew it. Now he had to face the music, the sheriff would be at the barn any minute.

It was at his point that Charles took off, except, no one knew that he had! They all thought he was still in the barn, being defiant to the law.

The Showdown

Within moments, Naperville's sheriff met Mrs. Hillegas in the front yard of her house. "Can you tell me again what is happening here, I didn't understand on the phone."
Mrs. Hillegas led the sheriff along the street and then pointed to her barn behind her house. "My son Charles recently lost his wife..."
The sheriff interrupted her, and shook his head in sympathy, saying, "I heard. Terrible thing. Terrible thing."
Mrs. Hillegas, frustrated, continued, "Yes. She died in Montana and Charles brought her back here to Naperville to be buried in our family plot in the Naperville Cemetery."
The sheriff nodded, "So I heard. She'll rest in peace there."
Mrs. Hillegas said, "Sheriff, he dug her up! They're in the barn! Both of them!"
The sheriff's eyes widened in disbelief, "The dead lady is in the barn?"
Mrs. Hillegas shook her head '*yes*'.
"God help us..."

The sheriff snapped into "sheriff mode" and quickly made his way to the barn while saying to Mrs. Hillegas, "Grave robbin' is against the law in these parts. Charley has done it this time." As he approached the barn he shouted to Charles, "Charley! It's the sheriff. I'll need you to come out of there, or I'm comin' in to get cha'." The sheriff waited a few seconds and then took a stance preparing to kick the door in.
Mrs. Hillegas grabbed his arm, warning, "He's got a gun!"
The sheriff turned to Mrs. Hillegas, "How do you know that?"
"When I saw them he was pointing it at me."
The sheriff backed away from the door. He rubbed the back of his neck to relieve the building tension, sighing, "That changes things. Don't want nobody killed over this."
By now neighbors began to gather around the area, curious about the commotion. They talked among themselves, saying, "I heard Mary tell the sheriff that Charley is in the barn with a gun." "Charley may be insane with grief, he lost his young wife last week, ya know."

The sheriff calmly rapped on the barn door to get Charles' attention, saying, "Charley, I don't want no more trouble here. I know what happened. Why don't you come out peacefully. I'll see that your wife is brought back to her grave all proper-like. What do ya say?"

There was no response from Charles.

The neighbors were in shock, asking, "His wife isn't in her grave?" "Where is she then?"

The sheriff asked again, "Charley? I need you to listen to me. You're in a heap of trouble and it's only gettin' worse. I need you to put down your gun and come out peacefully. Can you do that?"

There was no response from inside the barn. The sheriff was losing his patience. He motioned for Mrs. Hillegas to come near the barn door beside him. "Maybe you can talk some sense into him." Mary nodded in agreement.

She leaned in toward the door, "Charles? Son, I know you're scared. I know you're upset. I know how much you love Jessie. But she deserves to be at rest now. She can't find eternal peace in this old barn. We can help you if you'll let us. We can find a doctor for you. We can help Jessie by getting her out of this filthy barn and back to her resting place."

The gathering crowd let out a collective gasp. "Is his dead wife in the barn with him?" "That's what Mary said, I think." Several people, in shock, made the sign of the cross as they stood in horror at the macabre scene playing out before their eyes. "Dear God in heaven..."

Mary heard their gasps and murmuring. She turned toward them. She saw the vacant looks on their faces. Everyone involved was consumed with stunned disbelief. She had never known such shame, she turned back to the barn door, imploring her son, saying, "Charles, please, please end this nightmare. Please come out."

There was no response.

The sheriff motioned for Mary to join him, in the backyard, out of earshot of Charles and the growing group of spectators. "Look, the Hillegas family are pillars of our town, I know that, and I've tried to handle this as low key as possible to reduce the embarrassment of it for your family. But frankly, I'm afraid I have no choice but to bring in the county law enforcement. They ain't as understandin' as me. I'll give Charley another 40 minutes, till noon, to cooperate. If he ain't done so by then, he'll have to answer to the law of DuPage Country. I'm sorry Mary, but I got to keep the peace here, and frankly, I get nervous when an unstable man is unresponsive to the law, grave robbin', and waving a gun at his mother."

A tear rolled down Mary's cheek as she stared blankly forward and nodded in understanding.

The sheriff approached the barn door with new vigor and determination, shouting, "Charles? I need you to listen here. I've tried bein' patient with you, but it ain't workin'. Listen, grave robbing is a serious crime; you could see ten years of hoosegow for it. If you come out now, this whole mess can stay between the Hillegas' and the town, nobody else has to know about it. But, if I have to call in Sheriff Kuhn from Wheaton... Well boy, that's a new kettle of fish for you. We can do this easy-like, but I'll need you to come out. *Now.*"

There was no response.

I took this "forgiving" approach with the sheriff for this reason:

The "Naperville of old" protected "their own." This is evidenced by the fact that the local newspaper understandingly referred to Charles as "Grief Crazed," while the rival Wheaton Illinoisian paper called him a "Ghoul."

In addition, there are other examples in Naperville's history where they protected their own, such as the Bailey/Laird Murder of 1869...

It was January of 1869, Naperville Illinois. A man named Mr. Laird was caught in the wee morning hours entering the bedroom of a married woman named Mrs. Bailey – Mr. Laird was caught in the act by Mr. Bailey. Mr. Bailey promptly shot and killed Mr. Laird.

Was this a case of a dangerous prowler illegally entering a home to cause ill? Nope. Mr. Bailey had suspected that his wife and Mr. Laird had been having "private time." Of course, Mr. Bailey couldn't just walk up to Mr. Laird and shoot him – that's illegal. So, he told his wife that he had business out of town - so to give the lovers opportunity. Mr. Bailey then left on his journey, but, he returned unexpectedly, only to find Mr. Laird entering his home. Mr. Bailey shot Mr. Laird as a prowler, knowing full well that he had set Mr. Laird up to shoot him.

It was common knowledge that Naperville law enforcement looked the other way and considered the homicide justified. This was Naperville protecting their own, and it didn't go over well in surrounding cities. Consider for instance what the Chicago Tribune had to say: "Very likely the murdered man was a bad man, and the surviving woman a bad woman. Any other supposition makes this case altogether frightful. – [but] Who gave Mr. Bailey the right to take Mr. Laird's life?" And, "Any public sentiment which tolerates public killing is essentially barbarous and murderous. The consequences which follow such homicides are very grave."

Naperville law knew that Mr. Bailey had set Mr. Laird up, but they looked the other way...

Because of the Hillegas family influence, I believe the sheriff would have gladly swept this whole embarrassing debacle under the rug. Unfortunately, Charles' defiance left the sheriff no option other than to call in the county police, which, obviously, took the matter out of his hands. There is, however, a bit of irony here:

Charles wasn't being defiant – Charles wasn't responding to the sheriff because he wasn't in the barn! If the sheriff had known that fact, he wouldn't have had to call in the county police. Ultimately, it didn't make any real difference in the final outcome, even the DuPage County Law Enforcement yielded to the Hillegas family influence.

The Grave Robber Next Door

The huge crowd now knew for sure that Charles had been grave robbing. They knew that he had lost his reason, dug up his wife, and was now hold-up in the barn with her remains. This level of horror was like nothing else that had ever occurred in their town.

The story that Charles had robbed his wife's grave and tried to bring her back with his banana potion quickly moved through the "Naperville Gravevine," probably due mostly to the eyewitnesses who watched the spectacle play out.

The sheriff waited till noon, there was never any cooperation from Charles. He looked at Mary and sighed, "I'm sorry Mary. I'm callin DuPage." The sheriff returned to his office and notified the DuPage County Police, in Wheaton Illinois, of the situation. Within 30 minutes, DuPage County's Sheriff Kuhn arrived on the scene accompanied by City Marshal Ehinger and Deputy Sheriff Louis Graves.

The sheriff from Wheaton, Sheriff Kuhn, arrived at around 1pm, with Deputy Louis Graves, and City Marshall Ehinger. They immediately took control of the crime scene and discovered very quickly that Charles was no longer in the barn, this according to the Wheaton Illinoisian newspaper.

As promise by Naperville's sheriff, the county police were no nonsense. They circled the barn and told Charles that if he didn't come out peacefully they were coming in for him. They waited a moment for him to cooperate. He didn't.

Sheriff Kuhn drew his gun and brazenly kicked the barn door open. He jump inside and quickly surveyed the interior for Charles. He wasn't visible. There wasn't anywhere to hide. Jessie stood, partially standing, in the hay pile. He called out, "Hillegas? Where are ya?" The barn was silent.

"Is he here?" Asked Deputy Graves as he entered the barn.
The sheriff continued peering into every corner of the barn, concluding, "Doesn't appear so."
Graves walked up to Jessie's remains. "Holy mother of God..."
Kuhn approached. "OK. He's not here. That means he's armed, insane, and out on the streets somewhere. You and Ehinger check the house, he may be hiding in there. Don't bring the mom - He's still got a gun and if he starts firing I don't want her shot. I'll stay here with his unfortunate wife, in case he comes back. And Graves..."
"Yeah?"
"Make it quick. If he's not in the house, we've got just six hours of daylight left to find him."
Graves nodded and left.

Kuhn turned his attention to Jessie. He stared at her with disbelief. He sighed, "What kind of man would do this? And why?" That's when he noticed that there was some type of foreign substance on Jessie's mouth, face, neck, and dress. He reached out and scooped some onto a finger. He checked its consistency by rolling it between the finger and his thumb - slimy. He sniffed it - it smelled like banana. He looked at Jessie in repulsed befuddlement, asking, "What in God's name happened here last night?"

Sheriff Kuhn stood up and went outside the barn. A large crowd of spectators waited for any news. Mary Hillegas sat alone in a chair in the backyard, staring at the grass. He sat down in a chair opposite her. "Can I ask you something?"
Mary nodded, but didn't look up at him.
"Do you have any idea why your son might have fed his wife bananas last night?"
Mary looked over to him in confusion, "I'm sorry...?"
Kuhn cleared his throat for a second, to buy time to rethink the question. "Your son's wife, what is her name?"
"Jessie."
Kuhn nodded. "Jessie? OK. Do you have any idea why your son might have fed Jessie bananas last night? There was banana in her mouth, on her face, even on her dress. Any idea at all?"

"Banana's?"
"Yeah. There's no mistaking the smell of them. Any idea?"
Mary's eyes grew wide as she remembered the way the townspeople, six years ago, laughed about Harvey's claim to bring back the dead with an elixir he had - an elixir made from bananas. Mary realized the horrid truth: Charles was trying to bring Jessie back from the dead last night... She put her hand over her mouth, a chill ran up her spine, tears welled up in her eyes, her lip quivered, her mind was numb.
Kuhn noticed the sheer panic on her face, he asked, "So you know why?"
Mary had no intention of sharing the banana elixir tale. She answered, "No. I have no idea. Bananas? That's absurd." She turned away.
Kuhn knew she was hiding something. "Well, if you think of anything, maybe you could contact me."
Mary didn't respond.

Just then the two detectives came out of the house and into the backyard, Graves reported, "He's not in the house."
Kuhn looked to Mary, "Is there anywhere in particular you think he might have run off to?"
Mary just shook her head '*no*'.
Kuhn stood up and motioned for his detectives to follow him out to the street.
"We've got to find this guy. He couldn't have gotten too far, because, as far as we know, he's on foot. He probably left the barn right after the altercation with his mother this morning, so he's had a few hours head start."
Graves asked, "Where do we start?"
Kuhn nodded, "Well, he was born and raised here, so he knows the area like the back of his hand; if there's a place for him to hide, he knows where it is. Now, assuming that he stays on foot, he knows that if he goes south, west, or north, he'd be walking into farmland. That's a problem for him because he's no farmer. He won't fare well outdoors for long. If he heads east, toward Lisle, there's civilization. He'd be much more comfortable there. The easiest way to Lisle from here would be Chicago Avenue. We'll start there."

Because they found Charles so quickly they must have determined that Lisle was his destination and that he'd get there on foot via Chicago Avenue. It worked.

The detectives loaded into the car and headed east down Chicago Avenue toward Lisle. As they approached Dutter's Hill, about five miles east of downtown Naperville, they spotted a man, Charles' age, walking aimlessly along the road near an abandoned gravel pit. They pulled their car in front of him and exited.

As they approached him he said, "I knew when I saw the automobile that everything was up." Charles submitted quietly to his arrest. He was immediately taken to the jail in Wheaton, IL, the county seat for the town of Naperville.

Charles refused to give any explanation for his strange behavior.

This information, including the actual quote from Charles, is from the Wheaton Illinoisian account of the story.

Charles was arrested on suspicion of grave robbery, the penalty for which, if convicted, is one to ten years.

Ultimately, the Hillegas family cash and influence prevailed anyway and allowed Charles to walk away from this escapade with a proverbial slap on the wrist from a legal standpoint. We know this because there are no court papers of any kind on file with the county concerning this event and Charles' arrest, strongly suggesting that the whole thing was "swept away." Also, had Charles been sent to jail or a psych hospital he wouldn't have been active in Naperville so quickly following the crime. His family money and influence allowed him to simply spend a while under observation of a doctor.

In researching Charles' arrest we were shocked to discover that there isn't even an arrest record! There were no formal charges brought. There was no time spent in a psychiatric hospital such as the horrid Elgin State Hospital. The Hillegas family money and influence saw to it that Charles received only a proverbial slap on the wrist. Perhaps he knew that's how it would shake out.

The Hillegas family were good friends and neighbors of the Ellsworth family. And the Ellsworth family (namely, Louis Ellsworth Jr.) were very active and powerful in the local governments. This "Ellsworth connection" no doubt influenced the charges filed against Charles by DuPage County.

Epilogue

The Grave Robber Next Door

Charles Hillegas

Charles W Hillegas

Charles signature as it appeared on court documents, 1918

Following his arrest, Charles was examined as to his sanity. The following Monday he appeared before Justice of the Peace O. E. Higgins on the charge of Grave Robbing. He was absolved of all wrongdoing. He spent a few months in a private Chicago hospital under observation before being released and taking up residence on Chicago's south side.

That week, the newspapers of the day (Naperville's Clarion & Wheaton's Illinoisian) called Charles "Grief Crazed" and a "Ghoul." But, in typical Naperville fashion, there were never any follow up stories on the arrest or Charles in general. As far as Naperville was concerned, even to this day, this event never happened.

In January of 1918, a few months following the death of his mother, Charles initiated a lawsuit in the DuPage Court. He was suing his brother Harvey, his sister Ida, as well as the men who purchased Hillegas Hardware, all renters in the commercial building, and the renter of the Hillegas house on Front Street.

In this lawsuit, Charles felt that his family had sold him out and he wanted his share of the Hillegas estate. According to a story in the Naperville Clarion newspaper, Mrs. Hillegas sold Hillegas Hardware - this occurring just three months after the grave robbery. According to Charles' lawsuit, the men only rented the store and had overstayed their lease and he wanted his share of the rent money the money or he wanted them out. This is the second lawsuit initiated by Charles; the first being about a year after he and Jessie wed - Charles sued a local bank in Montana claiming they owed him $213. Copies of all documents are in the Appendix.

According to the U.S. census, in 1920 Charles was living on the south side of Chicago. He is a Lodger and listed as widowed.

According to the U.S. census, In 1930 Charles was living in Naperville, widowed, and renting a boarding room on west Franklin Street, in Naperville. The building no longer exists.

This census for 1930 shows Charles living on Naperville on west Franklin Street

In 1940, Charles died, alone, at 72 years old, in a wretched DuPage County Senior Living Facility, in Wheaton Il, on September 7th. Funeral services were held at 2:30 pm, on a beautiful Monday afternoon, at the Oliver J. Beidelman funeral home, on Naperville's Washington Street. The Rev. George Kurn officiated.

Received through his obituary in the Naperville newspaper.

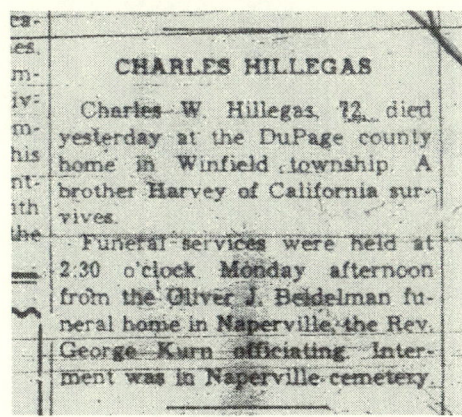

Charles resides in the Naperville Cemetery: Sec 3 Lot 944 Plot 11. Neither he nor Jessie have genuine tombstones, only cemetery markers. (See story: The Lost Graves)

Charles and Jessie never had children.

Jessie Hillegas

Jessie's remains were discovered to be unharmed when the authorities retrieved the body for reburial. However, folklore tells us that the Napervillians of the time quickly put two and two together and realized that the "Banana substance" found on Jessie was rumored to be the same life-giving Banana potion said to be housed at the Hillegas place. It was clear to everyone at the time that Charles dug up Jessie in an effort to bring her back to life.

This information is Naperville folklore.

Harvey & Jenette Hillegas

Harvey Hillegas had moved to California with his wife shortly after his father's death in 1906. He died at his home in Campo California on October 24th, 1943, after a short illness. His wife Jenette survived him. Although he had a place for burial here at the Hillegas family plot in the Naperville Cemetery, he chose to be interred in California. He resides in the Cypress View mausoleum in California.

Poor Harvey, his name was spelled wrong in his obituary. They spelled it Hilligas.

Summoned by Death

HARVEY H. HILLIGAS

Word has been received from Mrs. Jinnie Hilligas of Campo, Calif., of the death of her husband, Harvey H. Hilligas, on Oct. 24 after a short illness.

The funeral services were held from Merkally Austin parlors in Campo, Calif., on Oct. 28. Burial was in Cypress View mausoleum.

Mr. Hilligas who was born in Naperville and spent most of his life here, had many friends who will mourn his passing.

Harvey and Jenette had no children.

The Grave Robber Next Door

Mrs. Hillegas (Maria, Mary)

Mary Hillegas tried to continue running the affairs of Hillegas Hardware but that effort only lasted for three months. The newspaper says that she has been running the business since her husband's death in 1906 – they make no mention of her two sons helping her. In August of 1912, a few months are the grave robbery, Mary Hillegas sold the Hillegas Hardware store to several men who had been in business with her husband; Charles sued them in 1918.

NEW HARDWARE COMPANY

The Hardware Business established many years ago by Mr. Wm. Hillegas and which, after his death, was carried on by his widow, Mrs. Wm. Hillegas, has been sold and is now being conducted under the name of the Hillegas Hardware Company.

This Company is composed of Mr. E. E. Sargent, President and Treasurer, Mr. Chas. A. Rassweiler, Vice President and Mr. C. H. Tobias, Secretary, who, together with Mr. H. H. Rassweiler and Mr. E. Mertz, constitute the Board of Directors. All these gentlemen are financially interested in the business. Mr. Chas. Rassweiler has been connected with this business for the past nine years and Mr. E. Mertz for the past eighteen years.

It is the intention of the management to build up the stock of hardware and farm machinery and equipment so that all of their customers will find exactly what they want right in the store. In fact they propose to conduct a strictly up-to-date hardware and farm implement business. This will be accomplished as fast as the goods can be ordered and shipped in.

From August of 1912, just three months after the grave robbing

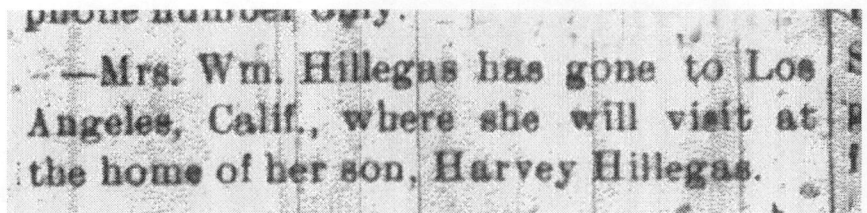

This appeared in the newspaper in October of 1912,
just five months after the grave robbing

Mary then moved to Los Angeles to visit her son Harvey. Once there, she decided to stay. She lived the last five years of her life in California, as far as she could get from Charles. She died at Harvey's house near San Diego California, at age 76, on January 4th, 1917. Her remains were returned to Naperville for interment at the Naperville Cemetery. Curiously, in life she ran away from Charles, but in death, she is buried right next to him. Her funeral was held on Friday, January 12th, 1917, at 2:30pm, at the First Evangelical Church of Naperville.

The First Evangelical Church of Naperville is the same Zion Church that Mary was married in. It is also the same church that provided the funeral services for her husband William. The church had changed its name.

Ida (Hillegas) & Simon Schaefle

Charles' sister, Ida, died on March 5th, 1948, in Maywood Illinois. She was the last surviving member of the family. She and Simon had five children (Ada, Mary, Cora, John, & Corinne). There are no grandchildren, so the William Hillegas bloodline stops.

After the shame of the grave robbing, and the lawsuit in 1918, Ida had very little to do with her brother Charles, in fact she isn't mentioned as a surviving family member in his obituary. Sadly, Charles died alone, as a pauper, in a decrepit senior facility, while his sister and her family lived just 30 miles away.

In addition, as the last surviving member of the Hillegas family it was probably Ida who updated the family plot with the current proper tombstones. However, she did nothing with the graves of Charles and Jessie. It was as if they didn't exist at all.

Ida's husband Simon died in 1941. Ida and her husband Simon, as well as a few of their offspring, reside in the Naperville Cemetery: Sec 3 Lot 944.

The Lost Graves
of
Charles and Jessie Hillegas

The Charles Hillegas story has so many intriguing facets. One of the most intriguing being that there is an account of the story (called the Gap Theory) that actually has Charles trying to reanimate his wife's remains 18 years after she was buried! A person doesn't have to work at CSI to know that 18 years in the ground is going to do major damage to a corpse. Certainly Charles would have found very little in Jessie's grave, let alone something that remotely resembled his wife or could be reanimated. One expert I talked to said Charles would be lucky to have found a few bits of bone and cloth. So how did such a crazy theory actually get "legs?" There are two pieces of evidence that if taken together paint the Gap Theory as the true Grave Robber story (even though it's completely impossible).

Wrong Evidence Piece #1) The fact that there is only one tombstone for a Charles Hillegas in the Naperville Cemetery. And the stone clearly states that his wife died in December of 1898. Here's the stone:

Wrong Evidence Piece #2) In the Naperville Sun newspaper, in the 1970s, an old man named Pete Schrader used to write a column reminiscing about old Naperville. Back in he early 1970s, Pete, then 81 years old, mentioned in a column that Hillegas robbed the grave in 1916.

Now, taken together, these two pieces of evidence erroneously tell us that the woman who was dug up was named Sarah; she died in 1898; and that her husband, Charles R. Hillegas, dug her up 18 years after he had buried her. Presto! - The Gap Theory. Unfortunately, none of it is true.

As Chuck and I embarked on the mission to dig up the true story of the grave robbing, one of our earliest projects was to check census records for the dates in question. It was here that we realized that the Charles Hillegas who lived on Ellsworth Street was Charles W. Hillegas, not Charles R. Hillegas - as was inscribed on the tombstone! That means the Gap Theory was referencing the wrong Charles Hillegas and wife! So, the death date of Sarah's, 1898, is irrelevant to the true grave-robbing story.

But here's the problem: The tombstone pictured above was the only tombstone in the Naperville Cemetery with the name Charles Hillegas on it! And we know he was buried in the Naperville Cemetery.

The Hillegas family that lived on Ellsworth Street in the late 1800s has a family burial plot in the Naperville Cemetery, but there were no stones in the burial plot for Charles or his wife.

Curious that we might be missing something, I took a short branch and started to stick it into the ground in between the Hillegas family tombstones. After a moment the stick hit something hard about 3 inches underground. Chuck quickly pulled the grass away and there was a marker that had sunken into the ground - a marker inscribed: Charles Hillegas. A few feet to the left there was another marker 3 inches buried, it read: Wife of Charles Hillegas. These markers are the graves of the grave robbing couple!

The hidden markers aren't actual tombstones; they have no birth/death dates for instance. As well, Charles' wife doesn't even have her name on hers. *But the markers are there.* Our opinion is that Charles so shamed his family with his grave-robbing actions that no one ever replaced the markers with genuine tombstones. In addition, the markers were allowed to sink into the earth to be forgotten forever. That is, until Chuck and I cleaned them off so Charles and Jessie could have proper graves.

The marker that reads: "Wife of Charles Hillegas" is marking the actual grave that Charles dug up that fateful night back in May of 1912...

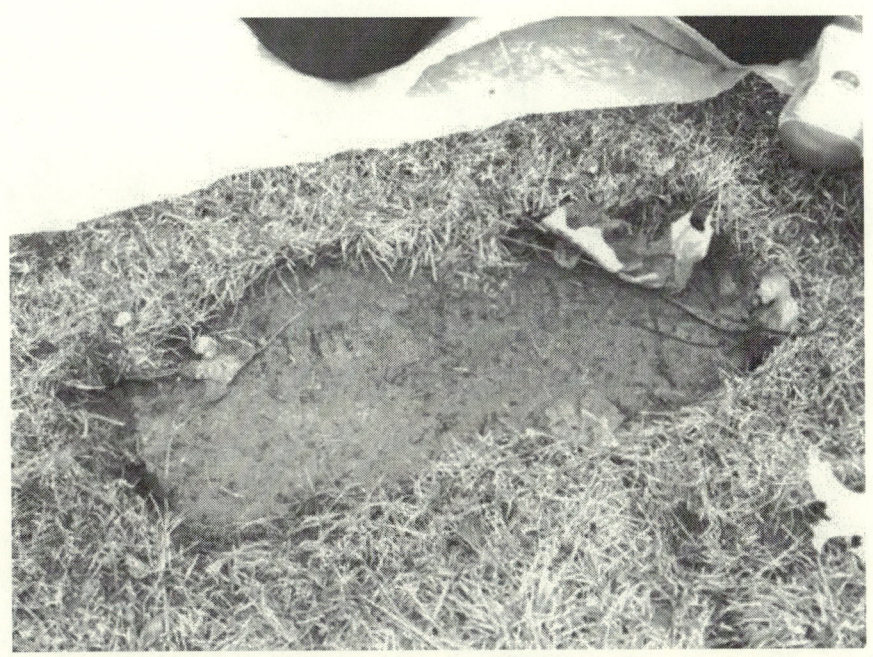

This is Charles' marker as it looked when we cut the grass away

This is Charles' marker after we cleaned it up a bit

This stone marks the grave of Jessie Hillegas; note that her name isn't on it.
This marks the actual grave that Charles dug up.

The Hillegas family plots before we discovered the lost graves of Charles and Jessie

The Hillegas family plots after the discovery of Charles and Jessie's markers

A Psychological Look at Charles and Jessie...

by

Dr. Chuck Kennedy

You may wonder how can we do a psychological profile on people who lived 100 years ago. How can we know enough about them to evaluate them? But the truth is we do know quite a lot about Charles and Jessie: We have their birth order; we have the fact that Charles is left handed; we have his signature; and we have their reactions to the circumstances they were in - all these traits are pieces of the "psychological puzzle." When we have two or more traits, we have Types. With two or more Types, we have a Profile. So let's see if we can build a Profile of Charles Hillegas.

We can start with the Birth Order Factor. Now how does that affect a profile? The birth order usually predicates a basic personality. Psychiatrist Alfred Adler (1870-1937) first proposed a theory on the effect of birth order on personality. Personalities are the way that we deal with all the tasks of life, including our professions, friendships and even ways that we entertain ourselves. Adler said that firstborn children are "dethroned" when the next child comes along and that they may never recover from that.

One must also consider the spacing between children, demographics, social status, changes in the household over the years, and the number of children that grow up in that house.

Curiously, if there is a gap between siblings longer than 6 years, you're looking at two different generations. For instance, if you have a sibling that is spaced at least that far apart from you, think about the different things the two of you discovered growing up—different music, technology, even world events. If you are living in the United States, you have seen many different presidents, different problems, and different celebrities. It's almost as if you have nothing in common at all, other than you're family.

Charles was a middle born of three children. The spacing was a few years apart so there were no generational issues. So lets take a look at Charles, a typical middle born. We know that middle born tend to be:

* People-pleasers

* Usually hate confrontation

* Basic need is to keep life smooth

* Their motto might be 'peace at any price'

* They are usually very calm

* Will 'roll with the punches'

* Down-to-earth

* Great listeners

* Are skilled at seeing both sides of a problem

* And eager to make everybody happy

* Tend to be less driven than first-borns

* They let others 'pave the way'

* Much more eager to be liked - or at least be happy with them

* They have a difficult time setting boundaries

* They are not good at making decisions that will offend others

* They will make promises that they have no control over keeping

* They also tend to blame themselves when others fail

* They will move mountains to try to make these failures right

* Able to accept personal strengths and weaknesses of other people

The Grave Robber Next Door

Now let's throw in Charles' signature and see what that tells us about him...

Charles N Lillegas

To start, the way he makes most of his letters, his C-H-A-L-E all indicate he is a good communicator. That would go with being a "peace maker," that we saw in the birth order. His signature is very legible indicating that he is, again, a good communicator. He's also logical and sociable. His baseline is extremely level indicating that he is honest, healthy, reliable, poised, self confident, and possesses self-control. He does not trail his last letters indicating that he is efficient, and careful. His letters are connected showing us that he has sound judgment, and is logical. Letter size is consistent telling us that he is self controlled and can tolerate monotonous tasks.

His pen pressure is light and consistent indicating that he is healthy and gentle. Lastly his letter spacing is tight and steady letting us know that he is organized and in control of himself.

We also know from his signature that he is left-handed. About 27% of the population is left-handed. In the 21st century being left-handed carries no social sigma, but remember: we're profiling someone who grew up in the late 1800s! Back then, "Lefties were different." They were taught that they were different. Many thought Lefties were in league with the devil, etc.

In addition, the world was made from a different perspective: tools, devices, everything was "backwards" as far as Lefties were concerned. We had to think very logically to be able to view things from their perspective and adapt accordingly.

Charles would have had to work around these obstacles in his daily life.

Let's take a look at Jessie...

From what we were able to learn, Jessie was the youngest in her family. She was born in England, in 1876. Her family moved to the U.S. when she was very young. At age 15 she was married-off to a man in Will County, Illinois. Divorced eight years later, she met Charles and they took off for Montana to start a new life together.

The youngest children, by birth order, tend to:

* Have strong people skills
* Love to entertain and talk to others
* Be energized by the presence of other people
* Not be afraid to take risks
* Get bored quickly
* Have a strong fear of rejection
* A short attention span
* When the fun stops, they've had enough
* To some extent they're self-centered
* They may harbor unrealistic expectations of finding a relationship that is always fun

Let's put all the pieces together...

The 16 personality types, which we'll use in our assessment of Charles and Jessie, are based on the well-known research of Carl Jung, Katharine C. Briggs, and Isabel Briggs Myers.

Of the 16 types of personality, we see that Charles fits into a type that is called: Extraverted Sensing Feeling Judging, or ESFJ.

The ESFJ tend to be warm-hearted, popular, and conscientious. They tend to put the needs of others over their own needs. They feel a strong sense of responsibility and duty. They value traditions, security, and serving others. They have a well-developed sense of space and function. Unfortunately, they often need positive reinforcement to feel good about themselves - it is labeled: "The Caregiver."

As an ESFJ, Charles' primary mode of living would have been focused externally, where he'd deal with things according to how he felt about them, or how they fit in with his personal value system. Charles secondary mode was internal, where he'd take things in via his five senses in a very literal, concrete, fashion. Charles would have been extremely good at reading others. He could see what needed to be done well before those around him noticed it. Charles would have enjoyed all types of tasks, and would have been good at anything he tackled. The ESFJ, such as Charles, often need approval from others to feel good about themselves. They sometimes have a hard time seeing or accepting a difficult truth about someone they care about.

So how does this fit our story? Well we know Jessie was a people person with a quest for new and exciting things and was easily energized by whoever was around her.

Charles was a pleaser, a confident, gentle, reliable, patient man who accepted responsibility for failure.

Now as the Grave Robber story goes: Jessie married young and divorced when it did not work out. When she met Charles, she was looking for fun, but feared rejection. Charles was a great communicator and eased her fears because he was so eager to please. They quickly fell in love. They fed off each other's energy. In their thirst for excitement they ran off to Montana. Life was perfect, till Jessie became ill. Charles fit the perfect profile as the caregiver - an older, loving, pleaser. He probably stayed by her bedside, dotting on her every need right up till the end. Then he blamed himself for her death. This was unbelievable, she was everything he ever wanted - now she was gone. He was overcome by grief. But, as an ESFJ, he was logical, intelligent, and responsible. There was only one choice and it was clear, he had to right this wrong. Remembering the conversation he'd had with his brother concerning a potion that was bringing chickens back to life, Charles had no choice but to take an impossible chance and give Jessie's corpse some of the potion.

In order to do that, he needed to get the potion, he had to take Jessie back to Naperville where the formula's recipe was. Upon arrival to Naperville, he was probably unable to locate the formula right away. But we know Charles is a patient, methodical man. He allowed the proceedings to take place. Jessie was buried in the family plot. Charles kept searching Mom's house for Harvey's notes on the chicken formula. After several days he finds it. He is now ready to give his bride her last shot at life. Charles heads down to the cemetery to exhume her remains. Busted, the cemetery caretaker catches him in the act. Charles is told he has to follow procedures and bring back the "paperwork" to dig her up. Charles is calm, he tells the caretaker, "I'll get the papers and be back." But, Charles is not delusional, he knows he can never get the paperwork to dig her up on a theory. So he waits, patiently. Two nights go by when he sneaks back to the cemetery under the cover of darkness. This time failure is not an option as he removes Jessie from her grave and bring her back to Mom's barn.

Was Charles crazy? It certainly appears not to be the case. A grief-stricken person in a psychotic breakdown would exhibit erratic thought patterns with a complete unorganized thought process. Charles was grief-stricken no doubt but he was anything but suffering a psychotic breakdown. Even if we take out the speculation and only look at the hard known facts – Charles made a conscious decision to bring her back to Naperville. He remained in control of her funeral; he was described as calm when he was caught trying to dig her up the first time; he calmly left to "get the paperwork." Now, had he been delusional at that time he would have approached the 'power's that be' and actually request the paperwork because he would have thought, in his delusion, that it was only logical to dig her up and feed her the potion. But, because Charles was thinking so rationally, he knew no reasonable person would buy that story. A delusional person thinks everyone will believe his or her reality. There was no Psychopathy to Charles' actions; Charles' only diagnosis at the time of Jessie's death was that he was in love.

Charles is a Teutonic word for the "strong one." Charles was trying to be strong for Jessie. When Jessie was sick, I'd bet that he made her a promise that he would not let her die – and he was trying to move mountains to keep his promise.

It is easy for the newspapers to paint him as mentally ill, to describe him as crazy. My only questions are these: If you were about to lose someone you love, and you had a one in a million shot to save them, would you take it? What would you do? How far would you go? I think to pass up a chance to save someone you love, exhibits a much greater illness than to go outside the box to try to save them.

Charles remained on this earth for 28 years after Jessie passed. He never remarried. I guarantee that every day for 28 years, Charles blamed himself for loosing Jessie. Not because he was mentally ill, but because that is the type of person he was.

Appendix

IN MEMORIAM.

MRS. MARY HILLEGAS

The life-story of a child of God is full of interest and inspiration. To recall and record the wonderful dealings of God, the many trials and struggles, the despairs and hopes, the joys and sorrows, the defeats and victories, is one of the most ennobling tasks of our lives. Every life is full of significance, the life of a Christian is supremely great. God alone can measure the value of a redeemed soul. When this life passes through the night, death, into the light of eternal day, we who are left on this side of the passage feel the pain of parting, and yet our sorrowful hearts are comforted for we know "at evening time there shall be light," and in that light all our big woes, all our life's struggles will shrivel into insignificance. How good it was that night came to this beautiful life, night, which was but the portal into eternal day, there to dwell in a temple that hath no need of the sun.

Mrs. Mary Hillegas, nee Hartman, was born in Lancaster, Penn., July 15, 1840. In her childhood she came with her parents to Illinois and lived in this city and its immediate vicinty ever since, with the exception of the last five years. The last years of her earthly pilgrimage she spent in the home of her son Harvey, in Monrovia, California.

On July 3, 1862, she was united in marriage to William Hillegas. This union was a most happy one. Three children were born to them, Charles W., Harvey and Mrs. S. M. Schaefle. Her husband preceded her in death eleven years ago.

Mother Hillegas was led to Christ in her early youth, joined the church, being a member of our Naperville First Church for more than sixty years. She possessed a strong personality, a sterling character, and a Christ-like life. In her religious experience she was positive, in her dealings with neighbors and friends upright, and in her home life, cheerful and lovable. To know her was to esteem and love her. She has a host of friends who are ready to pay her tributes of love and appreciation. Her life was full of ministries of love and kindness. But her course is finished, she has kept the faith, and has received the crown of life. Her late illness was of about six weeks' duration, but through all those days and weeks of sufferings she never complained, but was fully resigned to the will of her heavenly Father. In patience she bore her cross, being ready when the summons came to meet her Lord. Her weary marches have ended, she is at home with God.

"There is no death! what seems so is transition;
This life of mortal breath
Is but a suburb of the elysian,
Whose portal we call death."

She leaves to mourn her departure, two sons, Charles W. and Harvey; one daughter, Mrs. S. M. Schaefle; one sister, three grand-children, Mrs. Ada Moyer, Mrs. Carrie Rariden and John Schaefle, and other relatives, and a large circle of friends. We shall meet her again in the morning of the eternal day.

Photo of William as it appeared in his obituary, 1912

IN MEMORIAM.

William Henry Hillegas.

Born in Pottsville, Pa., August 4, 1840. Died in Naperville, Ill., April 29, 1900. Age 65 years, 8 months and 25 days.

He was the son of Joseph and Mary Hillegas who, with their family, came to this state in the year 1857 and settled on a farm near this city, the mother passing away three years afterward. Two sons died in the East, and two daughters departed this life after the family had resided in Illinois for some time, leaving a son, William H., and two daughters, Mrs. Edwin Rickert and Mrs. William Rubrecht, both widows now and residents of Naperville. The father, Joseph Hillegas, lived to be upwards of 90 years old, and was a respected citizen and a devout Chrstian.

The subject of this sketch developed in early life a liking for commercial activity and soon found an opening in the store of Andrew Fridley, the pioneer hardware merchant of Naperville. That he won by years of faithful service the entire confidence of his employer was shown by the fact that, in after years, in company with Louis Reiche, he became his successor, and later still sole owner; and no heart beat more sympathetically at the recent obsequies than did that of a son of the late Andrew Fridley—a comrade of youthful years.

On the 3rd day of July, 1862, he was married to Maria Hartman, daughter of Adam and Susana Hartman, both of whom lived to a ripe old age, their later years having been spent in this city.

To Mr. and Mrs. William H. Hillegas were born one daughter—Mrs. Simon M. Schaefle, and two sons—Charles and Harvey, who with their mother, and three grand-children—Ada, Carrie, and John Schaefle, are the immediate survivors of the paternal parent.

In the year 1864, as the demand for volunteers became very urgent, Mr. Hillegas enlisted and became a member of Company D, 156th Illinois Infantry, and served till the close of the civil war in 1865, receiving an honorable discharge. With him went many other young men from this town and vicinity, who can testify to his faithfulness as a soldier, maintaing his reputation as a Chistian under circumstances unknown in civil pursuits of life.

For nearly fifty years he was closely

For nearly fifty years he was closely and actively allied with the Evangelical Association as a member of the local Zion society, to which his loyalty never deviated and for whose welfare no sacrifice within his means was considered too great. In church and Sunday school work he was ever active, discharging his duties satisfactorily, quietly, pleasantly, expeditiously, and reverently. But the circle of his brotherhood was not confined to the members of his own church, but sympathetically embraced everybody who tried to live a righteous, honorable, upright life. He was as conscientious in his every-day dealings with his fellow men as he was sincere when he communed with his Maker in the private chamber or worshiped in the public assembly. His daily walk and conversation was a conspicuous testimony of his religious convictions. His predominating motto through life—"Better suffer wrong than do wrong"—was strictly followed.

In the year 1876 Mr. Hillegas was elected trustee of the village board, serving one year with W. L. Good, Otto Sieber and Charles Boettger as associates, Hon. Lewis Ellsworth being the president during that term.

As a business man Mr. Hillegas was moderately successful. But he, too, like every other merchant upon whom constant demands are made outside of the ordinary course of trade, had to pass through financial trials which test men's courage and powers of endurance and frequently leave physical wrecks and shattered fortunes on the shores of time. That he weathered the storm, maintained his integrity and met every obligation was due to his faith in God, backed by an unconquerable determination to win. And win he did, maintaining to the last the unbounded respect and confidence of every man who knew him.

But the end came entirely too soon. The brittle strand was severed almost without warning. The constant daily grind of forty years' duration brought to a sudden close a busy, useful life. On Saturday night, April 28, he was taken ill, and about 24 hours later his spirit was released, leaving only a tenement of clay as a reminder of the departed occupant.

The funeral took place from the home on Thursday, April 3, partly under the supervision of Walter Blanchard Post, G. A. R. of which the deceased was a member. Some forty comrades served as pall-bearers and escort. The floral tributes were appropriate, varied and beautiful. The attendance at Zion church was large, embracing representatives from every church and society. Brief addresses were delivered by Revds. Hinsey, Umbach, Klingbeil and Manehart, interspersed with vocal selections. At the grave, the Grand Army burial service closed the obsequies of one who will long be remembered as a genial friend, a loyal husband, an indulgent father, a respected citizen, a devout Christian, a conscientious merchant, a faithful soldier, an honest man—an example worthy of imitation by the rising generation.

WIERD ACT OF A GRIEF-CRAZED MAN

Naperville citizens were shocked yesterday morning when the report was circulated that Charles Hillegas had disinterred the body of his dead wife in the Naperville cemetery, had taken it to the barn at the home of his mother on Front street and was defying any interference with his plans.

Mr. Hillegas had brought the remains of his wife from Seattle, Wash., last week Monday for burial here. It was evident that his mind had become unbalanced from the strain of grief and the long journey alone from the west, and on the night of her burial he claimed to have had a vision that his wife was still alive and he proceeded to the cemetery and was discovered in the act of uncovering the newly made grave at that time.

Since then he has been carefully watched, but on Monday night he again went to the cemetery and succeeded in removing the body of his dead wife from the grave and coffin and bringing it back to Naperville with him.

Tuesday afternoon Sheriff Kuhn came from Wheaton and took charge of the case. Shortly after one o'clock he, with his deputies, went to the Hillegas barn where Charles was supposed to be armed and guarding the remains. Upon entering the building it was discovered that he had fled, but the remains were found unharmed.

Later, Mr. Hillegas was found walking east on the Chicago road at Dutter's hill. He was taken to Wheaton where he will be examined as to his sanity.

As published in the Clarion newspaper
May 15, 1912

WHEATON, DuPAGE COUNTY, ILLINOIS, FRIDAY, MAY 17, 1912

DUG UP WIFE'S BODY WHILE SEXTON SLEPT

Grief Crazed Ghoul Removes Body to Barn and Stands Guard

IS IN SHERIFF'S CUSTODY

Prisoner Had But Recently Returned from the West Where He Had Spent the Past Twelve Years

After exhuming the body of his dead wife from its resting place, in a Naperville cemetery, Charles Hillegas, driven temporarily insane, stood guard over her body, which he had removed to a barn in the rear of the Hillegas home at that place, and brandishing a gun, defied the citizens for many hours last Monday morning.

Sheriff Kuhn was immediately notified of the man's strange actions, and accompanied by City Marshal Ehinger and Deputy Sheriff Louis Graves, hastily repaired to the place.

Hillegas, who is thought to be

VICTIMS OF MEASLES NOW NUMBER FORTY

Epidemic Which Started Last Saturday in South Side School, Still Spreading

The epidemic of measles which seems to have had its inception on the South side, according to City Physician, Dr. J. H. Rasch, has spread through other quarters of the city, until now there are more than forty known cases.

Dr. Rasch, when seen yesterday, in speaking of the spread of the disease, said:

"You can say for me that, according to my best belief, the members of the First grade class of the South school, numbering about forty, seem to have been exposed to infection more than two weeks prior to the time it broke out in Miss Hull's class. Today there are but eight out of the forty pupils still attending school, and several cases have been found in various quarters of the city.

"Many people are grumbling because the Board of Health has seen fit to quarantine all cases of measles, but the State Board of Health requires it, therefore I am powerless. Measles are by no means severe, and those cases already noted are of a particularly light character.

"I have not thought it advisable to close up the schools for the reason that the children have already been exposed, and practically some of them are left who have not already had

Hillegas, who is thought to be about 40 years of age, recently returned to his former home at Naperville accompanying the dead body of his wife, whom he had wedded somewhere in the West. It is thought that her death had preyed upon his mind until he lost his reason.

Last Saturday night the sexton of the cemetery found him digging up the freshly laid earth over his wife's grave and, suspecting that the man was not right, informed him that it would be necessary to obtain a permit before the body could be removed from the grave. Hillegas left, saying he would soon return with a permit. Again Monday night he stealthily entered the cemetery, this time evading the sexton's watchfulness. After breaking open the casket containing his wife's body and using the cover of the rough box for a litter, he transported the body to his mother's barn, where he stood guard over it throughout the remainder of the night.

Early the following morning, his mother, suspecting that her son's absence augured ill, went to the barn in search of him, and was horrified when she saw the body of her son's former wife resting in a partly standing position, against the cover of the rough box.

Early the following morning, his mother, suspecting that her son's absence augured ill, went to the barn in search of him, and was horrified when she saw the body of her son's former wife resting in a partly standing position, against the cover of the rough-box.

She hastily notified the authorities, who in turn notified Sheriff Kuhn. Accompanied by City Marshal Ebinger and Deputy Sheriff Louis Graves, the party began their search for the missing man, who was finally overtaken near an abandoned gravel pit five miles east of Naperville. He submitted quietly to his arrest, saying:

"I knew when I saw the automobile that everything was up."

He was immediately brought back to Wheaton and placed in jail.

Hillegas is said to be a highly educated man, and is the son of one of Naperville's wealthiest hardware merchants.

He refuses to give any explanations for his strange behavior, and is held to appear before Justice of the Peace O. E. Higgins next Monday, charged with grave robbery, the penalty for which, should he be convicted, is from one to ten years.

Now that you know all about Charles and Jessie,
it's time to *visit them*.

Kevin's **Ghost Tour of Naperville** runs every weekend, and the Hillegas location is one of our most haunted tour stops!

Check us out online at:
HauntedNaperville.com

Or call: 630.205.2664

Yes, Kevin personally hosts every tour.

Looking for
Ghost Tours
and
Ghost Hunting
Excursions
in the Chicago Suburbs?

Visit us online:
GhostsOfIllinois.com

Dr. Chuck Kennedy is your host
for dozens of
spirited adventures.

*"Don't let your weekend be normal,
make it paranormal!"*

Kevin's seminar:

"How to NOT Become a Ghost"
is the
Hottest Ticket in town!

Held in libraries all over the Midwest, this 2-hour program lays out the four steps you can take in your life to substantially reduce the chance that you become a lost and miserable earth-bound ghost.

Details at:
HauntedNaperville.com

Kevin's book:

Naperville, Chicago's Haunted Neighbor

Is available at:
HauntedNaperville.com

Dr. Kennedy's book:

Neural Psychology and the Paranormal Investigation

is available at:
GhostsOfIllinois.com

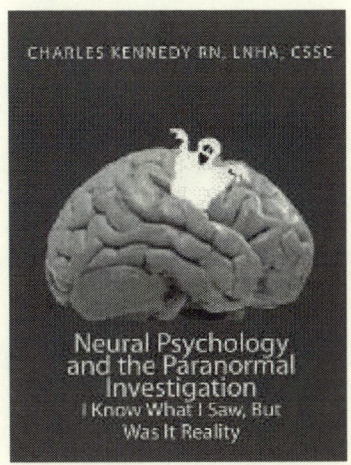

Made in the USA
Charleston, SC
04 May 2012

Zimring, Franklin E. (1998b) "Juvenile Justice Reform: The Youth Violence Epidemic: Myth or Reality?" in *Wake Forest Law Review*, 33: 727–44.

Zimring, Franklin E. (1998c) "Youth Violence: Toward a Jurisprudence of Youth Violence" in *Crime and Justice*, 24: 477–500.

Zimring, Franklin E. (2000) "Penal Proportionality for the Young Offender: Notes on Immaturity, Capacity and Diminished Responsibility" in Thomas Grisso and Robert G. Schwartz (eds.), *Youth on Trial: A Developmental Perspective on Juvenile Justice*, Chicago: University of Chicago Press, pp. 271–89.

Index

aberrant
  behavior 51–3
  cases 52
  crime 54
  defense 51–3
  failures 52
  nature of juvenile crime 46
  psychological mechanisms 46–7
abortion 30
Ackerman, Bruce 146n.13
acquittal 31
actions 10, 12, 16, 20, 22, 47, 66, 71, 104, 106,
    110–13, 118, 126, 130, 135, 145, 148–9,
    151–2, 163–5, 177, 180–1, 191, 219
  authorized by the law 16
  citizen-affecting 148
  generation 47, 123
  legal reasons 125, 127, 134, 136
  of legislators 97
  permissible 13, 66
  properties 66
  unjustified 14
acts 52, 66, 68, 75, 78–9, 82, 91–2, 98, 101, 104,
    115, 118, 121, 126, 134, 215, 218
  autonomous 164
  charitable 68
  citizen-affecting 148
  criminal 68, 90, 158, 201
  evidences 93–5
  expressive 167
  features 72, 123, 126, 129, 135, 137–9, 142,
    144, 148
  from normal psychological capacities 47
  impulsive 6
  in conformity with legal rules 136
  in deliberation 103
  in the presence of peers 45
  in violation of norms 67, 68, 72–3
  manifesting psychological states 96
  moral features 127, 132n.7, 138
  moral wrongdoing 136, 138
  moral wrongfulness 139–40
  of anointing by law 132
  of assigning reason-giving weight 110
  of defrauding 133
  of false verification 131n.6
  of prosecutorial discretion 2
  of restraining movements 170
  of robbery 107–8, 122
  of violence 111–12, 122
  pain-causing 71, 77, 105–6, 129
  performed neither from compulsion nor
    ignorance 14–15
  place in the space of reasons 15, 102–3, 119
  prohibited 80, 136, 138, 142, 188, 201
  reason-giving properties 103
  supported by reasons 70, 106–7
  that cause harm 118
  that drive deliberation 71
  that favor the child 42
  that fulfill parental obligations 41
  token 68, 72, 109, 128
  types 68, 81, 119, 127, 142
  unsupported by reasons 70
  see also wrongful acts
adjudication 2, 91, 176
adolescence 45n.1, 53
adolescents 2, 4, 20, 36, 44–5, 179
adult
  citizens 189–90, 197
  criminals 2, 4, 9, 18, 23, 53, 82, 158, 183,
    204–5
  life 51
  offenders 205
  population 196
  prison 3, 208
  role models 39
  system 2–4
  visitors and immigrants 187, 189, 195
adulthood 45nn.1–2, 49, 174
adults 1, 3–7, 9–12, 14, 16–20, 22, 26, 28, 31,
    42–7, 49–50, 52–8, 61–5, 82, 97, 99, 125,
    145, 150, 158–9, 167–75, 178–82, 184, 187,
    197, 203–9, 211–12, 214–17, 219–20
  enfranchised 84, 159, 164, 185–6, 188,
    190, 200
  immature 183
  interrogation 210–11, 214
  mature 183
  psychological profile 51
  teachable 5
aesthetes 78
aesthetic
  norms 67, 72
  reasons 127–8, 134
affective states and dispositions 104–5
age 6–7, 13, 17, 21, 24–6, 31–4, 39, 46, 48–9, 51,
    55, 57, 168–9, 178, 180, 204, 214, 217, 220–1
  and opportunity 25
  categories 181

age (*cont.*)
  for voting 8, 11–13, 17, 172
  gap 204
  groups 31, 38
  inequality 36
  limits 178
  of culpability 40
  of maturity 12, 50
  of puberty 31
  of the defendant 211
  of the offender 1, 13
  political meaning 125, 159, 195, 216, 219
  proxy 27, 33, 66, 173–4, 218
  qualifications 181
  standards 35, 49
  threshold 16, 27–30, 33, 35, 173–4, 176, 178–82, 218, 220
agency 122, 163, 165
agents 14–15, 68–9, 71, 74, 80, 82, 94, 96, 99, 102–7, 110–11, 116, 121, 124, 143, 147, 151, 153, 156, 158, 193, 199, 218
  behavior 59, 80
  complicity 164
  culpability 68, 80, 154
  developmental stage 57
  ideal 102–4, 107–9, 111–15, 118–19, 122–4
  modes of recognition 70, 71, 95, 106–7
  modes of transaction 71–3, 77, 79, 83, 87, 90, 95
  psychology 104–5
  rational support 104
  relation with token act 68
  say over the law 75
  wrongful conduct 24
airport safety 36
alcohol/intoxication 34, 74, 95
American
  adults 167
  citizens 143
  fiscal policy 160
  government 146n.13
  kids 180
  law 143–4, 180
  legal system 88, 155
  soil 144, 191
  see also United States
American Civil Liberties Union (ACLU) 185n.1, 196n.5
antipsychotic medication 68–9
Aristotle 14, 82
Arpaly, Nomy 70n.4
assault 54
atrocities 46
attorneys/lawyers 1, 139–40, 149, 154, 201, 206, 209–10
Austin, John 129

background 93–5, 103
  constraints 93
  construction 88–90
  facts about groups 91
  information 85–7
  norms structuring 86
  propositions 86–90, 97
  structure 88
  theory of human behavior 90
Baltimore 215
behavioral
  capacities 158
  differences 4, 8, 17, 97, 159
  duplicates 10
  goal 56
  properties 12
  similarity 182, 195, 207, 209, 215
  smoke 18
  twins 182, 201, 204
benefits 27, 29, 34–6, 41, 60, 100n.4, 140, 151, 162, 169, 196, 208
Berman, Mitchell 120
Blackstone's Ratio 31
blame 5–6, 8, 14–15, 23n.6, 100n.5, 171
blame-reducing features 7
blameworthiness 5n.10, 6–8, 13
boys 4, 31, 34–6, 38, 51, 86, 218
brains 30, 179
  of children 18
  of immature adults 183
  of kids 10, 18, 182
brain science 18, 20
break, *see* giving kids a break
Brink, David 22n.3
burdens 27, 35–6, 41, 68, 100, 140, 161, 213, 219
burglary 204, 210, *see also* larceny, robbery, theft
Bush, George 196
Buss, Emily 30n.10

California 132, 148, 173
California Penal Code 80–1, 130–1, 133
Carroll, Jenny E. 19n.1
cases
  Afroyim v. Rusk (387 U.S. 253 (1967)) 198n.6
  Almeida-Sanchez v. United States (413 U.S.266 (1973)) 190n.3
  Bluman v. FEC (800 F.Supp.2d 281 (D.D.C. 2011)) 189–91
  Brown v. Entertainment Merchants Association (131 S.Ct.2729(2011)) 170
  Craig v. Boren (97 S.Ct 451(1976)) 34
  Ginsberg v. New York (390 U.S.629(1968)) 169n.3
  Graham v. Florida (130 S.Ct.2011 (2010)) 2n.1, 46

INDEX 233

Hazelwood School District v. Kuhlmeier
  (484 U.S.260 (1988)) 169
In Re Gault (87 S.Ct.1428 (1967)) 3n.2
J.D.B. v. North Carolina (131 S.Ct.2394
  (2011)) 210–15
Lamb v. Brown (456 F.2d 18 19(10th Cir.
  1972)) 31n.11
Miller v. Alabama (132 S.Ct.2455(2012)) 2n.1,
  20, 23n.4, 28–9, 62, 205n.2
Miranda v. Arizona (86 S.Ct.1602(1966))
  210n.8
Montgomery v. Louisiana (136 S.Ct.718
  (2016)) 205n.2
Montgomery v. Louisiana
  (577 U.S.__(2016)) 2n.1
Roper v. Simmons (125 S.Ct.1183 (2005)) 1,
  2n.1, 19, 65n.14
United States v. Carolene Products (58 S.
  Ct. 778) 181
United States v. Carroll Towing Co. (159 F.2d
  169 (2d. Cir. 1947)) 213n.10
Wong Wing v. United States (163 U.S.228
  (1896)) 190n.3
causal
  connections 96
  contributions 163
  links 90
  powers 106
  relations 69, 84, 96–7
  responsibility 68–73
  sense 164
  transactions 84n.17, 85
causation 68–9, 84, 92, 96–7
censure 47–8, 74
Chang, Ruth 208n.4
character 60, 79, 88, 206
child 2, 6, 18, 41–2, 49–50, 168, 170–1, 174
  abuse/molestation 83, 137, 138
  criminals 3–4, 5n.10, 9–10, 12, 55, 182–3,
    203–5, 208, 219, 221
  development 215, 217
  interrogation 209–10
  leniency 11, 211
  psychology 16
  speech 169–70
  suspect 206–7, 211, 215
childhood 44, 49
  abuse 5, 82–3, 168
  deprivation 5, 39, 82–3
  influences 179
  nature 3
  trauma 74
children 1, 5, 9, 14, 17, 19n.2, 20, 22, 23n.6, 31,
  42–3, 45, 48, 50, 55–6, 65, 83, 98, 117, 138,
  168–71, 174, 178, 183, 185, 189, 197, 200–1,
  206–7, 209, 211–12

behavior 168, 174–6
brains 18
character 20
diminished in culpability 10–11
disenfranchisement 173, 179
distribution 175
education 42, 168–9, 174
intrinsic features 10
sexual offenses against 204
values 16, 175–6, 178–82, 184, 220
vulnerability to harm 169
China 160
Cillessen, Antonius H. N. 45n.2
citizen-affecting actions/acts 148, 152
citizens 1, 15, 98, 108, 116, 129–30, 144, 146,
  152, 163–4, 166, 180, 188–92, 194–8, 218,
  220
  autonomous agency 165
  complaints about state actions 163
  enfranchised 185–7, 190, 193, 220
  having a say 146, 148, 150–1, 159, 163–5,
    167, 172, 176, 196
  law-abiding 15, 44, 55, 92
  status 15, 84
citizenship 15, 83–4, 143–4, 156, 188, 190,
  198n.6
classification 29, 32–4, 36–8, 87
Clinton, Hillary 181, 196
clubs 146–8, 161–2
Code of the Aesthete 78
coherence 197–9, 201, 220
Cole, James 139n.9
Coleman, Jules 132n.7
comparative proportionality principle 35
complicity 70n.3, 152–3, 163–4, 168, 171,
  188–9, 219
  in government/state action 10, 16, 163–5,
    171, 176–7, 219
  in judgments 151–2, 189
  in legal norms 189, 219
  in the law 191–3, 195, 199, 201–2, 219, 221
compulsion 14–15, 82–3, 156
condemnation 138, 146
  expressed by legal institutions 141
  expressed by the law 139, 143–4
  of behavior 138–40
  of conduct 139
  of crime 51
  of simple possession 154
conduct 11, 23, 40, 46–7, 72, 76, 78–9, 81, 83,
  89–90, 92, 95, 104–10, 112, 120–1, 131–2,
  136, 139–40, 151, 153, 156, 163n.2, 189,
  213, 221
  criminal 21, 45, 54, 88, 97, 99, 158, 194
  domains 30
  heinous 1, 74, 76

conduct (*cont.*)
  illegal 218–19
  legally authoritative 168
  morally egregious 134
  morally impermissible 134
  norms 31n.12, 68, 73, 77
  prohibited 15, 51, 147, 188
  see also wrongful conduct
confession 87, 210, 213
conviction 3n.2, 31, 40, 206–7
courts 1–3, 20–1, 28–9, 34, 46, 56–8, 62, 64–5, 87n.19, 169–70, 181, 189–91, 198n.6, 203, 205–6, 210–12, 214–15
crime-producing settings 20, 23
crimes 1, 10, 12–13, 16, 18, 30, 34–5, 44, 50–4, 56–7, 59–64, 66–7, 81–2, 84, 88, 92, 99, 114–17, 122–3, 125, 134, 137–41, 143, 145, 151, 155, 158–9, 162, 164, 171, 182–3, 185–7, 190–1, 196–8, 200–1, 205, 207, 210, 214–15, 217–19
  by adults 2, 9, 12, 23, 28, 53, 183, 205–6
  by disenfranchised prisoners 187
  by illegal immigrants 186
  by juveniles 4, 46
  by kids 2–3, 5, 7, 10, 18, 23, 29, 44–6, 48, 53–5, 58, 61, 75, 82, 158, 171, 182, 203, 205, 219–20
  by prison inmates 197
  by visitors 190
  definitions 204
  mala in se 75, 77
  non-mental elements 80
  of negligence 52
  of violence 46, 54, 183
  reduction 59–60
criminal
  culpability 10–18, 23, 35, 66, 68, 70n.4, 72, 75–80, 82–4, 88–92, 117, 125–6, 134, 153–4, 156, 158, 162, 201, 217–18, 221, *see also* culpability, Proxy for Culpability argument
  justice system 18, 56–8, 140–1, 203
  liability 1, 4–8, 10, 12–13, 17–18, 52, 80–1, 151, 171, 185–7, 191, 195, 197–202, 217, 219–20
  prohibitions 51–3, 68, 151, 164, 188, 201
criminality 56, 137, 155
criminalization 7, 9, 51–2, 76, 139, 170, 204n.1, 216
criminogenic
  circumstances 23–4, 52
  condition 13
  dispositions 125
Crook, Shirley 1
culpability 7, 15, 22n.3, 28, 34–6, 40, 47, 66, 68, 70, 72, 74, 79, 83–4, 87, 93–5, 101, 117–19, 124, 155, 159, 171, 182, 197, 204, 206, 213
  as modes of transaction with reasons 71
  assessment 19, 88, 91, 97, 212
  differences 13
  diminished 10–11, 16, 66, 82, 171, 200
  for *mala in se* crimes 75
  moral 20, 70–3, 75–6, 83, 88, 91, 156
  reduced 11–12, 18, 99, 125, 182–3, 218–19
  standards 15, 84
  theories 14–16, 73, 78, 96–7
  see also criminal culpability, Proxy for Culpability argument
Cunningham, Milagro 46, 75–6

death sentence/execution 1–2, 9, 46, 59, 67
decision-makers 89
decision-making 30, 33, 180
defendants 2, 3n.2, 20, 26, 51, 54, 64, 81–2, 89–90, 92, 108, 131, 141, 154–5, 158, 183, 201, 204–7, 211, 213, 217
Delgado, Richard 23n.5
deliberation 70–1, 103–8, 111–13, 118, 158–9
democracies 8, 88, 129, 148, 166–7, 185n.1, 202
desert 16–17, 98, 101–3, 114–15, 120, 124, 155–6, 171, 182, 197, 200
  as isomorphism in the space of reasons 102–3, 107, 119
  comparative 116
  concepts 99, 102, 117
  differences 117–18
  for blame 100n.5
  for criminal behavior 125, 154
  for wrongdoing 10, 15, 66, 98–100, 109, 124, 126, 153, 158, 218
  intuitions 101
  legal 109
  moral 108–9
  non-comparative 119
  of criminal punishment 99
  of criminal sanction 162
  of harm 112
  of punishment 218
  ordinal 102, 109, 113, 119, 122
  relationships 117
  rhetoric 196
  theory 100–1, 116–17, 122
deterrence 58–60, 122–3
developmental
  curve 28
  normality 10, 13, 21, 44–50, 53–5, 57–9, 65, 125, 183
  processes 63
  psychology 18, 50–2, 54–5, 57–9, 182–3
  stage 2, 56–7, 169, 181
DiIulio, John 4
disenfranchisement 1, 17, 182, 184–5, 198, 201–2
  of felons 17
  of groups 17, 186–8
  of kids 3, 66, 168, 171, 173–4, 180, 184, 201

of prisoners 187
of protestors 160
of the poor 201
of visitors 199
on the basis of age 174
domestic violence courts 57
drug
  courts 57–8
  trafficking 141
dualism 124
Duff, R. A. 9
duplicates 10, 97, 158
duress 10, 54, 183

earthquakes 68–70, 84
Ebbesen, Ebbe B. 56n.9
education 42, 56, 60, 65, 168–9, 174
elections 85, 129, 160, 167, 196
empirical
  assumptions 26, 29–30, 33, 36, 174
  challenges 46
  claims 4, 29–30, 46, 48–9, 181–2
  dependency 29–30, 33–4, 39, 41–3, 48–9, 51
  discoveries 33, 43, 48, 50, 218–19
  error 5, 61
  evidence 32
  grounds 46
  premises 48
  problem 208
  questions 16, 31–2, 36, 63, 206–7, 212
  research 13
  support 32, 45
  work 19
enfranchisement 172–4, 179–80, 202
  of adults 17, 84, 164, 169, 185–6, 188, 190, 200, 220
  of citizens 185–7, 190, 192–3, 220
  of inmates 198
  of kids 181
  of the poor 201
  of those with a criminal past 201
epistemic
  credentials 89
  merit 86, 88
  norms 86
epistemology 85–6, 88–9
equality 31, 88–91, 93–4, 165, 174–5, 178–9, 181, 190–1, 195
evidencing 85, 95
evidentialist theory of manifestation 84, 90, 92–6
exclusionary reasons 38–9
excuses 6–8, 14, 80–1, 183, 188
  of compulsion 14, 82–3, 156
  of ignorance 11n.15, 14, 82–3, 156
  of mistake 10
  status 15, 83–4, 156
execution, *see* death sentence/execution

Fagan, Jeffrey 23n.5
fair opportunity 24–6
false negatives 27–8, 30, 32–3, 37, 39–40, 48, 172, 179, 218
false positives 27–9, 31–3, 37–41, 173, 218
felonies 54, 107, 140, 196, 201
felons 17, 185, 187, 196, 198n.6
films 77–8, 168–9
Finders Keepers 131
fines 57–8, 67n.1, 99, 122, 139
Finkelstein, Claire 207n.3
Fischer, John 77
fitness 88, 98–101
Florida 46, 196
freedom 3, 72, 116, 188

gender 31–6, 39, 86–8
gender-sensitive policy 31–40
girls 4, 31–2, 34–6, 38–9, 46, 51, 75, 86, 218
giving kids a break 3–5, 7–8, 10, 12–14, 16–20, 22, 23n.6, 24, 26, 28, 30–3, 35–6, 38–44, 47–51, 54–5, 58–60, 64–6, 98–9, 101, 124–6, 151, 156–9, 163, 171, 182, 185–7, 190, 197, 201–3, 205, 208, 215–19
Gore, Al 196
governance 88, 184, 197, 202
government 12, 88, 116–17, 138, 146n.13, 148, 160–1, 166–8, 172, 175, 178, 185–6, 188, 190–2, 194, 196, 198–9, 202–3, 210, 220
  actions 10, 16, 152, 163–5, 219
  activity 36–7
  behavior 19, 27, 29, 32, 164, 176, 197
  failure 32–3, 211
  functions 37
  misconduct 87
  moral obligations 76
  participation 44
  property 114–15
  see also self-government
graffiti 3, 54, 136
Gray, Freddie 215
Greenberg, Mark 128n.2
Guantanamo Bay 163
guardians 168, 170, 184, 206
guilt 3n.2, 31, 37, 40, 80, 87, 89, 107, 130, 206

Hand formula 213
harm 4, 6–7, 15, 19n.2, 34, 42, 52, 76, 86, 91–3, 98–101, 112, 114, 118, 134, 149, 158, 168–71, 178, 200, 207–8, 213, 217
Hart, H. L. A. 35n.14, 129
having a say 16, 146–54, 159–70, 172, 174–80, 182, 184–5, 187–9, 191–2, 194, 197, 199, 218–20
Hawaii 173
height-sensitive policies 32–3, 40
Hershovitz, Scott 128n.2

INDEX

Hobbes, Thomas 145
Holder, Eric 139, 154
homicide, *see* murder/homicide
Hume, D. 96
Husak, Douglas 11n.15, 52n.5, 77n.7

ignorance 11n.15, 14–15, 82–3, 156, 213
immaturity 6, 18, 183, 219
immigrants 185–7, 189, 191, 220, *see also* visitors
indictment 140, 143, 147
inequality 35–6, 165, 167, 175–7
infants 2, 169
injustice 7, 12
inmates, *see* prisoners/inmates
innocence 31, 37, 40, 54, 87, 89, 206
insiders 144–5, 148, 150
institutional
  behavior 8, 147
  conceptions 136
  measures 147
  strength of legal reasons 140–3, 148–9, 154
institutions 10, 140–2, 159, 171, 184, 220–1
interrogation 17, 203, 208–11, 213–16
intuition 1, 34, 39, 69, 98, 101, 116–17, 122, 124, 186–7, 197, 212, 215–16
Iraq 180, 196
isomorphism in the space of reasons (ISR) 102–4, 106–7, 109, 114–24

jail, *see* prison/jail
Japan 143–4
J.D.B. 210–16
Judaism 31n.12
judges 17–20, 53, 61–4, 88–9, 92, 97, 115, 166–7, 201, 204–7
judgment 29, 61–4, 75–6, 92–4, 98, 102, 108–9, 113–14, 150–2, 189, 197–8, 212–13
juries 1, 3, 88, 206, 217
jurisprudence 14, 132, 156–7, 190
jurisprudential
  foundation 126
  theory 125, 129, 132, 134, 156
  views 157
justice 4, 16–19, 28, 37, 44, 87, 101, 124, 182, 198, 216, 221
juvenile
  crime 4, 46
  detention 208
  offenders 20
  standard 212
  system 2–3, 56, 204–6, 217
juveniles 2, 4, 46, 56, 205, 207, 209, 211, 215

Kids Will Be Kids argument 21–3, 44–51, 54–5, 64–5, 125, 159
  experimentation defense 51, 53–4
Kim Jong-un 76, 78

larceny 107, 109–10, *see also* burglary, robbery, theft
lawyers, *see* attorneys/lawyers
legal
  positivism 125–32, 135–6, 144, 155–6, 193
  reasons 10–16, 66, 72–3, 75–6, 80–2, 84, 89–90, 97, 99, 112, 115, 125–59, 161–2, 164–5, 171, 182–3, 187–8, 190–3, 195, 197, 200–1, 210, 213–16, 218–19
  systems 13, 53, 78, 88–9, 126, 132, 137, 143–5, 150, 155, 158, 165, 216, 220
legislators 41, 97, 129, 176
leniency 2–3, 5–7, 9–14, 16–17, 22, 44, 52, 59–60, 64–5, 75, 83, 124–5, 150, 159, 171, 182–3, 186, 191, 195, 198, 200–5, 211, 216, 218–21
lenity 89–91, 93–4, 108, 155, 158, *see also* Principle of Lenity
Lerner, Craig S. 5n.9
Lewis, David 107n.10
lex talionis 123–4
Leydet, Dominique 145n.12
life without parole (LWOP) 2–3, 20, 60–4, 205, *see also* parole
littering 102, 114, 119, 122, 138
Locke, John 145

Maine 185n.1, 196
Makepeace, Jamaine 114–15, 117
mala in se crimes 75, 77, 99
Manza, Jeff 185n.1
marijuana 139, 149, 154
marshmallow test 55–6
maturity 6–7, 12–13, 20, 31, 47, 49–50, 55, 183, 219
McKenna, Michael 100n.5
Meares, Tracey 23n.5
medication 68–9, 84
mens rea 7, 14, 19n.1
mental
  disability 14
  disorder 14, 83
  properties 127
  representation 105
  states 117, 119, 123, 158, 183
Mexico 180, 198
Michigan 107
Mill, John Stuart 145
Miranda warning 210–11, 213–15
Mischel, Walter 56n.9
mitigation 6, 8, 82, 216
  in sentencing 7, 17, 53, 203–6, 208, 220
Model Penal Code 92
modes of recognition of reasons 70–3, 80, 89, 94–5, 105–9, 111, 113–14, 121, 124, 153
modes of transaction with reasons 14, 70–4, 79–84, 87–91, 93, 95–7, 105, 114–18, 123, 153–4, 156, 158–9, 164, 182

INDEX

money laundering 140
Moore, Michael 14, 83, 84n.17
morality 71, 91–2, 108, 127, 129, 131, 134–5, 161, 193
Morse, Stephen J. 7n.13
Mother Theresa 68
motivational states and dispositions 104–5
murder/homicide 1–2, 6, 46, 54, 67, 82, 99, 122

Nash, Ogden 53
natural law 125, 135–6
neuroscience 18–19, 45, 182–3
New York 22, 114, 188
non-epistemic norms 86–9
North Korea 76
Nozick, Robert 101n.6

obscene material 169–70
offenders 1, 4, 7, 9–10, 13, 20, 28, 36, 54, 57, 61–4, 188–9, 205, 208, 214, 216
Oklahoma 31
oppression 17, 37–9, 159, 185–6
outsiders 51, 144–5, 150
Owens, David 163n.2

pain-causing acts 77, 105n.9, 106
parental
  consent 169–71, 187, 189, 218
  efficacy 178
  entitlements 175
  gating 16, 171, 187
  influence 179–80
  liability 168
  obligation 41
  presence 209
  responses 6
  treatment 110
parents 13, 16–17, 41–2, 65, 110, 168–71, 174–82, 184, 187, 206, 210
parole 2–3, 20, 60–4, 185, 196, 205, 211, *see also* life without parole
paternalism 56, 58
pawnbroker 80–1, 130–3, 148
peer influence 11, 23–4, 26
peers 6, 20, 45, 174–5, 178
penalties 2, 7–9, 46, 114, 133, 139, 149, 205, *see also* sentences
Pereboom, Derk 98n.1
personhood 14–15, 83, 143, 156
philosophers 5n.10, 9, 82, 99, 156
philosophical
  argument 186
  discourse about criminal law 67
  error 4–5
  issues 17
  machinery 16
  rationale 4

theories 10, 21, 98, 117
work on the nature of responsibility 14
philosophy
  of law 9, 126, 208
  of punishment 9, 122, 208
  of the nature of childhood 3
  political 145–6
police 17, 110, 203, 206–16, 220
poor/poverty 17, 39, 88, 167, 186, 198–202
positivism, *see* legal positivism
poverty, *see* poor/poverty
precocious children/kids 5nn.9–10, 28, 48–9, 183, 200, 219
Principle of Legality 75–6, 81
Principle of Lenity 89–90, 93, 108, 155, 158, *see also* lenity
prisoners/inmates 56–7, 163, 185, 187–8, 196–8, 202, 220
prison/jail 2–3, 17, 57–9, 61–2, 67n.1, 99, 102–3, 114–16, 119, 121–2, 187, 196–7, 205, 208
probation 58, 185, 187, 196, 208
prohibited 82, 122, 131, 137, 154, 163
  acts 72, 80, 127, 130, 134–6, 138, 142, 188, 201
  behavior 16, 52, 80, 149
  conduct 15, 51, 125, 136, 147, 218
  see also criminal prohibitions
proportionality 35, 61–2, 116, 117
prosecution/prosecutorial 2, 75, 131, 140–1, 143, 206
prosecutors 2, 18, 139–41, 154
Proxy for Culpability argument 21–4, 25n.7, 28, 31–5, 37–43, 45–51, 54, 66, 125, 159
  empirical assumptions 26, 29–30, 36
  see also criminal culpability, culpability
psychiatric testimony 94
psychological
  capacities 13, 24, 29, 43–5, 47–9, 55, 158, 172–3
  commonality 174
  development 2, 217
  differences 8, 11, 19, 82, 96–7, 159, 182–3, 195, 207, 209, 215
  diminishment 200
  dispositions 105, 125
  effects of poverty 200
  features 11, 28, 43, 66, 105–6, 209, 218–19
  frame of mind 10
  harm 200
  identical 17
  immaturity 219
  mechanisms 44–55, 57–9, 123
  profiles 28, 51
  properties 12
  states 11, 13, 20, 24, 29, 47–9, 95–6, 101, 105, 117–18
  twins 201, 204

238   INDEX

psychology 4–5, 7–8, 10–11, 16, 18–20, 43, 45, 89, 96–7, 104, 106, 116–18, 182–3, 186–7, 195, 202, 209
punishment 1–3, 5, 7–10, 12, 15, 29, 34–6, 38–9, 44, 46–7, 51, 53, 56–63, 65–6, 75–6, 80, 81n.13, 82, 98–9, 100n.5, 101, 107, 114, 116–20, 122–3, 135, 137–9, 141–3, 146, 151–4, 164, 168, 183, 187–96, 201, 203–9, 216–18

quality of will 77–9

race 4, 33, 36–8, 71, 88, 111, 172
rape 26, 38, 46, 75, 99, 123, 134, 137, 140
Raz, Joseph 38, 132–3
reason-giving
 facts 70, 79, 105
 force 14, 72–3, 89, 96, 107, 111–12
 power 126
 properties 103–4
 weight 60, 71, 73, 77–82, 90–2, 94, 106–8, 110–16, 118, 123–4, 133
reasons-responsiveness 77–9
recidivism 56–7, 61, 198
religion 31n.12, 36, 71, 126–7
restitution 102
retributivism 35, 101, 117, 119–20, 123
robbery 26, 99, 103, 107–10, 112, 121–2, *see also* , burglary, larceny, theft
Roberts, Justice John 46
Rousseau, Jean-Jacques 145

sadist 105–6
sanctions 7, 10, 15, 44, 49, 141, 146, 154, 158, 162, 171, 182, 200–1
Sarch, Alex 70n.4
Scanlon, Thomas 77
Schapiro, Tamar 5n.10
Scheres, Anouk 45n.2
schools 56, 86, 169, 173, 210–12
Schroeder, Timothy 70n.4
self-government 16, 174, 176–81, 184, 197, 220
self-incrimination 87n.19, 206, 210
sentences 1, 4, 9, 17, 20, 53, 58, 60–4, 82, 109, 114, 130, 185–6, 196, 201, 203–8, 217, 220, *see also* penalties
sentencing 1–2, 7, 17, 53, 61, 203–6, 208, 216, 220
Shapiro, Scott 129n.4, 130n.5
Shelby, Tommie 201n.7
Shoemaker, David 6n.11
Simmons, Christopher 1, 6, 9, 11, 21, 46, 54, 59–60, 65
Singapore 188, 189n.2, 191–2
slogans 5, 135, 168
South African apartheid 172
speech protections 16, 159–60, 167–71, 187–90

stare decisis 89, 179
statutes 14, 16, 34, 52, 54, 80–1, 89, 108, 125, 128, 130–1, 133, 136–41, 143–5, 146n.13, 148–50, 154, 170, 173, 204
Steinberg, Laurence 29–30, 53n.7
stereotypes 34–5
Strawson, Galen 74n.5
Strawson, P. F. 77
strength of a legal reason 12, 15, 135–42, 144–7, 149–50, 155–6, 158
super-predators 4
supervenience 127–32, 136–40
Supreme Court, *see* United States
Syria 144

Tadros, Victor 79n.12
taxes 132n.7, 142, 198
Taylor, Jakaris 46
Taylor-Thompson, Kim 19n.1
theft 14, 51, 54, 72, 80, 102, 114, 123, 128, 130, 137, 151, 216, *see also* burglary, larceny, robbery
They'll Grow Out of It argument 21–3, 45, 55, 59–65, 125, 159
Thomas, Justice 170
Tiboris, Michael 5n.10
toddlers 2, 124
trials 1, 3, 190, 206–7
Trump, Donald 196
trustworthiness 27
truth 8, 24–6, 43, 86–7, 102, 121, 131, 164, 193

Uggen, Christopher 185n.1
United States 2–4, 12, 137–8, 143, 146, 149, 163, 167–8, 173, 176, 180, 182, 185, 188–91, 196, 204n.1, 206
 Congress 162
 Democrats 85
 Department of Justice 139n.9
 Fifth Amendment 87n.19, 210
 First Amendment 169–70, 189–91
 Liberals 145, 188
 Republicans 145–6, 151, 188–9
 Sentencing Commission 57
 Supreme Court 1–2, 17, 20–1, 34, 46, 62, 65, 87n.19, 169, 181, 190, 198n.6, 203, 205, 210
 Transportation Security Administration (TSA) 36, 39
 see also American

Vermont 139, 185n.1, 196
violence 4, 46, 54, 57, 76–7, 107–12, 169–70, 183, 201
visitors 17, 144, 159, 185–95, 198–9, 201, 220, *see also* immigrants
Von Hirsch, Andrew 48, 50n.4, 53–4

votes/voting 8, 10–12, 16, 41, 85, 129, 146, 159–62, 166–8, 171–5, 177–83, 185–8, 190, 192, 196–202, 204, 218–20
   age 8, 11–13, 17, 173, 179, 182

Walker, Nathan 46
walk the line 55, 57–8
Ward, Cynthia 19n.2, 23n.6
Washington, George 176
Water, Erik de 45n.2
Watson, Gary 14, 82
Westen, Peter 213n.9
Williams, Bernard 104–5
Wisconsin 196
wrongdoers 6–7, 15, 23, 35, 50, 56–7, 100, 116–17, 124, 131, 152

wrongdoing 5–6, 10, 15–16, 47, 56–7, 59, 66, 68, 75–7, 83, 88, 96, 98–103, 109, 114, 116–17, 119, 124, 126, 134, 136–8, 151, 153–4, 158, 204, 218
wrongful
   acts 7, 15, 24, 50–1, 66–8, 70–2, 77, 80, 87–8, 96, 99–100, 102–3, 107–8, 114, 117, 122, 127, 130, 136, 139, 151–3, 158, 188
   behavior 6, 13, 16–17, 21, 23, 40, 42–3, 49, 59, 74, 99, 115, 125, 130, 140, 200
   conduct 7, 14–15, 22, 24, 29–30, 45, 47, 50, 55, 59, 73–4, 100, 115, 125, 188, 206, 218
wrongfulness 22, 24, 66–8, 71–3, 77, 136, 138–40, 152, 188–9, 215

Zeiss, Antonette Raskoff 56n.9

Made in the USA
Middletown, DE
26 May 2022